NEW DIRECTIONS FOR INSTITUTIONAL RESEARCH

J. Fredericks Volkwein, *State University of New York at Albany*
EDITOR-IN-CHIEF

Larry H. Litten, *Consortium on Financing Higher Education,*
Cambridge, Massachusetts
ASSOCIATE EDITOR

Quality Assurance in Higher Education: An International Perspective

Gerald H. Gaither
Texas A&M University

EDITOR

D1509145

Number 99, Fall 1998

JOSSEY-BASS PUBLISHERS
San Francisco

QUALITY ASSURANCE IN HIGHER EDUCATION: AN INTERNATIONAL
PERSPECTIVE
Gerald H. Gaither (ed.)
New Directions for Institutional Research, no. 99
Volume XXV, Number 3
J. Fredericks Volkwein, Editor-in-Chief

New Directions for Institutional Research is indexed in *College Student
Personnel Abstracts, Contents Pages in Education,* and *Current Index to Jour-
nals in Education* (ERIC).

Microfilm copies of issues and chapters are available in 16mm and 35mm,
as well as microfiche in 105mm, through University Microfilms Inc., 300
North Zeeb Road, Ann Arbor, Michigan 48106–1346.

ISSN 0271-0579   ISBN 0-7879-4740-7

NEW DIRECTIONS FOR INSTITUTIONAL RESEARCH is part of The Jossey-Bass
Higher and Adult Education Series and is published quarterly by Jossey-
Bass Inc., Publishers, 350 Sansome Street, San Francisco, California
94104-1342 (publication number USPS 098-830). Periodicals postage
paid at San Francisco, California, and at additional mailing offices. POST-
MASTER: Send address changes to New Directions for Institutional
Research, Jossey-Bass Inc., Publishers, 350 Sansome Street, San Francisco,
California 94104-1342.

SUBSCRIPTIONS cost $56.00 for individuals and $95.00 for institutions,
agencies, and libraries.

EDITORIAL CORRESPONDENCE should be sent to J. Fredericks Volkwein,
Institutional Research, Administration 241, State University of New York
at Albany, Albany, NY 12222.

Photograph of the library by Michael Graves at San Juan Capistrano by
Chad Slattery © 1984. All rights reserved.

Printed in the United States of America on acid-free recycled paper containing 100 percent recovered waste paper, of which at least 20 percent is
postconsumer waste.

CONTENTS

EDITOR'S NOTES

Quality has become a major international issue for the academy as higher education has found itself under increasing scrutiny, primarily from governments, from the media, and from consumers concerned about receiving greater value for their investments. In Chapter Eight of this volume, Anthony Adam and Malcolm Morrison present an extensive international bibliography of published, unpublished, and Web site materials about quality assurance policies and procedures in individual countries. Trudy Banta (1997), an astute observer of this landscape, has written about the similarities among nations as they have adopted such systematic measures as quality assurance systems. She uses an analogy of concentric circles to explain the approaches commonly used. In the outermost circles are national systems of quality assurance, followed by regional and state systems, then campus and discipline-specific programs—with all quality assurance efforts beginning as well as ending in the classroom, at least theoretically. This scheme reflects one of the international iron laws of quality assurance: academic quality is best maintained and improved when responsibility for it is located as closely as possible to the institutional processes of teaching, research, and service. The creation of a successful quality assurance program, then, should be viewed primarily as a professional issue, not as an external political or internal administrative function. In the final analysis, quality is best maintained and enhanced through the professional commitment of the faculty, not through quality assurance systems, controls, or legislation.

Highly correlated with these international trends is a growing concern on the part of the public and policymakers with decentralization, "reinventing" government, and pushing review and evaluation efforts back down to the more basic level of classroom operation. This is a healthy trend if faculty respond with a strong sense of professional commitment. Therein lies the rub, however. Historically, the professional interests of faculty have been a force for continuity and organizational status quo. Clark Kerr's observation (1987) about faculty a decade ago could arguably still be applied worldwide: "One must be impressed with the endurance and the quiet power of the professorate, and particularly of the senior professors, to get their way in the long run—and that way at all times and in all places is mostly the preservation of the status quo in terms of structure and finance" (p. 186). The concerns of politicians and the public about faculty unwillingness to respond are not new. What is different— very different—now is the environment in which the concerns are being expressed. In many countries, the intersection of increased competition for public funds and rising enrollments will virtually require adoption of some form of quality assurance system by the academy to ensure social and fiscal support.

During the 1990s, governing bodies have begun to give institutions more autonomy in exchange for increased evidence of accountability. There is also growing evidence that these efforts are improving performance and efficiency better than centralized controls. (See, for example, MacTaggart and Associates, 1996, 1998.) For example, the current Dutch Model, discussed by Peter Maassen in Chapter Two of this volume, indicates that the faculty's clear ownership of the system, rather than the central government's heavy hand, has made continuous quality improvement a dominant feature of the Dutch system; a delicate balance between internal improvement and external accountability is maintained by a responsive faculty who accept the legitimacy of the system. An international review shows that the most successful quality assurance processes are those that start with an institutional self-audit, perhaps using standardized procedures, followed by verification by an external body. As noted earlier, successful quality assurance is a regular and progressive feature of professional commitment, and a continuous, active, and responsive process. The objectives of the institution become the starting point, as well as the terminating point, for such a self-audit. The self-audit compares quality processes and outcomes with objectives, and actions are taken to remedy the discrepancies.

The sharing and dissemination of good practices and the adoption of innovative ideas are central to maintaining peak performance in the best quality assurance systems. Yet despite the similarities among global themes and pressures, only limited information on quality assurance efforts is available, particularly from an international and comparative perspective, to guide a search for enlightened policies and practices. The purpose of this volume is to present some of the best quality assurance policies, practices, and procedures (and their philosophical grounding) found in five progressive countries—the United States, England, Scotland, the Netherlands, and Spain—and to offer an international set of resources and recommendations to assist practitioners in achieving the goals of their own quality assurance frameworks.

The Language of Quality

As quality has become a major issue in the academy, it has become necessary to introduce a new lexicon (new at least to higher education) for dealing with its various aspects. This terminology is used throughout the case studies in this volume to describe and discuss the issues involved. I have relied heavily on the *New Zealand Universities Academic Unit Manual* and on the works of David Woodhouse, the director of this unit in Wellington, in preparing the definitions that follow. The conciseness, clarity, and lucidity with which this unit and its director set out the definitions and operating processes and procedures related to quality are exemplary.

The distinctions among such terms as quality audit, quality assessment, quality assurance, and accreditation may be somewhat murky to the sophisticate, and downright confusing to the neophyte. Yet perhaps the lexicon of quality is more helpful than it appears at first glance. The following definitions will clarify some of the more common terms used in the chapters ahead.

Quality. *Quality* has many interpretations, as E. Grady Bogue points out in Chapter One of this volume. One definition is that a quality object is "exceptional" in some sense. By implication, therefore, most things are not of high quality. The consumer and the public, however, expect products of high quality to be generally available, and the understanding of the term *quality* is changing, partly as a result of public expectations. For example, the public is unlikely to continue to accept the idea that a high-quality education is exceptional, but such an education should indeed be the norm. Thus, the term *quality* is being redefined because of rising expectations of graduates' attainments.

Quality Assurance. *Quality assurance* has been defined as "the policies, attitudes, actions and procedures necessary to ensure that the quality of education and scholarship (including research) is being maintained and enhanced. It includes checking that the [quality control mechanisms, processes, techniques, and activities] are in place, are being used and are effective. It requires actions internal to the institution, but may also involve actions of an external body or bodies. It includes course design, staff development and the collection and use of feedback from students and employees" (New Zealand Universities Academic Unit, n.d., Chapter Two, Web version). In industry, quality assurance is a managerial task. However, as noted earlier, in academia it is a professional faculty issue that requires professional commitment, generally of a nonauthoritarian, nonadministrative nature. External participants as well as internal professionals are involved in internal quality assurance processes that should be continuous, active, and responsive. Effective quality assurance in the academy requires the use of external points of reference, both national and international. Publications such as this one can lead the reader to such points of reference.

Quality Audit. A *quality audit* is a review of the quality assurance and quality control procedures of an institution that includes a sampling process to see if the procedures are working. The term is commonly used to refer to any quality assessment that attempts to measure outcomes. The focus of a quality audit is on an institution's processes, with the institution's objectives serving as both the starting and terminating point of the audit.

Quality Assessment. The aim of *quality assessment* is to assign a grade to the quality of an institution or department through the use of an external evaluation process (see Chapter Five by Chris Carter and Alan Davidson for a discussion of its use in Scottish higher education). The outcomes of research and teaching in a given department or discipline are commonly assessed and graded separately. The assessments are typically carried out by observation, interview, performance indicators, and the examination of student work. Quality assessment may be criterion referenced, tying it to absolute standards or to the department's or institution's own goals or specifications. It may also be norm-referenced with comparisons across disciplines or institutions.

Accreditation. The meaning of the term *accreditation* differs somewhat from country to country. In the United States, accreditation typically consists of certification by a regional or professional accreditation body (such as engineering or law) that a program or institution has a generally recognized and appropriate set of goals and objectives that are being achieved. Goals and standards can vary with institutional mission. In some countries, such as Nigeria and China, the goals are referenced to a precise external set of criteria. In other countries, such as Hong Kong, the goals and objectives are more general, internationally recognized standards for a particular level of qualification. In all cases, accreditation is carried out by an independent body external to the institution.

The preceding definitions, while limited, are intended to help the reader grasp the subtle distinctions found in the various concepts related to quality. Quality assurance is mainly an internal phenomenon, whereas accreditation is always carried out by an external body. Quality audit and assessment are also generally carried out by external bodies, although internal approaches are commonly a valued part of the process. Finally, a major trend in quality management is toward quality enhancement, moving beyond mere measurement and maintenance. This expanding concept is intimately related to changing the definition of *quality,* as noted earlier, as well as to government and consumer concern about receiving greater value for their investments. Finally, these efforts are increasingly focused on efficiency goals and not on learners.

Methodology

Using case studies of individual countries and their educational systems, the authors of this volume provide a wide range of standards, proposals, and practices at different stages of development. In the review and evaluation of various national systems of quality assurance, as in the study of individual personalities and cultures, the investigation of a single case (nation) remains one of the best means for revealing the wholeness of a system or process in action. These national case studies show how particular components—history, culture, political structure, problems, and opportunities—participate in the international pattern of similarities and interrelationships among the various countries, and how these countries adapt best practices to their particular situation. A general knowledge of the inner dynamics of particular systems and of the relationship of those systems to outside events and problems will also help the reader to form a basis for review and planned change in other, comparable national (or local) systems of quality assurance. What is more, such national case studies can help immediately to lift the reader to a higher level of realism and sophistication.

Chapter Seven demanded a certain amount of prescience and has required the editor to take some prophetic risks in an effort to anticipate the role and directions that quality assurance efforts will take in the upcoming millennium.

Acknowledgments

This volume was originally conceived and indirectly sponsored through several projects on performance indicators and accountability supported by the Fund for the Improvement of Postsecondary Education (FIPSE). I am particularly indebted to Frank Frankfort, my program officer, and to Charles H. (Buddy) Karelis, the director of FIPSE, for the support and resources they provided for the preparation of this volume. The opinions expressed by this author and his colleagues are not necessarily those of FIPSE, and no endorsement should be inferred. Also, Jeanette Williams, my staff assistant, and Tony Adam, my research assistant, made numerous sacrifices to help prepare this volume. I also thank Larry Litten, at the Consortium on Financing Higher Education, and the staff at Jossey-Bass, particularly copyeditor Alice Rowan. Finally, I would like to thank the chapter authors for their contributions.

Gerald H. Gaither
Editor

References

Banta, T. W. "Further Steps Toward Globalizing Assessment." *Assessment Update,* 1997, *9* (6), 3, 15.

Kerr, C. "A Critical Age in the University World: Accumulated Heritage Versus Modern Imperatives." *European Journal of Education,* 1987, *22* (2), 183–193.

MacTaggart, T. J., and Associates. *Restructuring Higher Education: What Works and What Doesn't in Reorganizing Governing Systems.* San Francisco: Jossey-Bass, 1996.

MacTaggart, T. J., and Associates. *Seeking Excellence Through Independence.* San Francisco: Jossey-Bass, 1998.

New Zealand Universities Academic Unit. *New Zealand Universities Academic Unit Manual.* New Zealand Universities Academic Unit, n.d. (Web version).

GERALD H. GAITHER is director of institutional effectiveness, research, and analysis at the Prairie View A&M University campus of the Texas A&M University System.

Quality assurance in higher education is an activity as much personal as systemic, as much moral as technical. Effective quality assurance in colleges and universities is built on thoughtfully crafted systems and on the caring and courage of those who hold those learning climates in trust.

Quality Assurance in Higher Education: The Evolution of Systems and Design Ideals

E. Grady Bogue

Is the quality of an educational program or institution to be found in its reputation or in its results, in rigor of process or in proof of outcome? Is the purpose of quality assurance systems to encourage educational improvement or to demonstrate accountability and stewardship of resources? How can a society honor its egalitarian motives, with an accent on opportunity, while simultaneously honoring its commitment to excellence, with an accent on high standards?

Will the definition of *quality* allow a consideration of precision and art, numbers and beauty? Is quality to be found in the eye of the beholder, or in the judgment of peers? Is quality by definition in limited supply, or may it be found in any program or institution that is meeting its goals? Is a culture of evidence complementary to a culture of responsibility and trust? Is the assurance of quality primarily a matter of well-designed systems and technical processes, or does it depend as much on the compassion and courage, the moral and ethical posture, of those who give voice and meaning to our colleges?

These questions reflect the challenges inherent in defining, developing, and demonstrating quality in colleges and universities. The purpose of this chapter is to explore the best thought and practice on these questions and to enhance understanding of quality assurance in colleges and universities. Given the complexity of higher education's purpose, history, and culture in different nations, this is not an easy task. We begin by exploring several theories of quality, then move to the evolution of quality assurance systems, and finally suggest a set of design ideals on which the pursuit of quality in college and university settings

NEW DIRECTIONS FOR INSTITUTIONAL RESEARCH, no. 99, Fall 1998   © Jossey-Bass Publishers

might be founded. Let us commence the journey of understanding more about the question of quality by exploring definitions and theories.

Theories and Definitions of Quality

In business and corporate sector conversations we may encounter several definitions of *quality,* including the following:

Conforms to specifications. A product or service that meets design specifications is a quality product or service (Crosby, 1984).

Is fit for use. A product or service that satisfies the customer's or client's expectations is a quality product or service (Guaspari, 1985).

Achieves its mission and goals (program or institutional effectiveness). An individual or organization that achieves its goals is a quality program or institution (Green, 1994).

Improves continuously. An organization that creates a climate for constant improvement is a quality organization (Deming, 1986).

Considers multiple factors. Quality is a multifactor concept involving not only fitness for use but also reliability, durability, esthetics, and so on (Garvin, 1988).

Let us press the theme further. It may be an oversimplification for colleges and universities but one can think about the concept of quality from three perspectives. One of these perspectives assumes that by definition quality is in limited supply—a competitive affair in which there are a few truly excellent institutions. A second perspective assumes that quality should be present in each and every institution according to its mission and goals. A third perspective assumes that quality is to be found not in resources and reputations but in results, in the "value added" by the institution.

The Theory of Limited Supply. Certain conventional assumptions are widely held by academics and by friends of higher education:

- Only high-cost colleges have quality.
- Only large and comprehensive colleges have quality.
- Only highly selective colleges have quality.
- Only colleges with national reputations have quality.
- Only colleges with impressive resources have quality.

One of the earliest rankings of college quality in the United States was a 1964 study by Allan Cartter. Logan Wilson's foreword to Cartter's report contains this arresting opening line: "Excellence, by definition, is a state only the few rather than the many can attain" (p. vii).

Is collegiate quality in finite supply, a commodity of scarce availability? The assumptions just listed can produce a pyramid of prestige in which larger colleges and universities reside at the apex of the quality tetrahedron while less prestigious colleges and two-year community colleges occupy the lower levels. In the United States one can find this theory at work in the yearly rankings and ratings of America's "best colleges" according to *U. S. News and World Report*. In the Netherlands, the Higher Education Inspectorate, a government entity, advises the minister of education and offers rankings of Dutch universities that reflect this approach (Palmer, 1995).

The Theory of Quality Within Mission. An alternative to a pyramidal structure of quality—an order of prestige and reputation built on size, selectivity, and program diversity—is a system in which we see the potential for high quality in a variety of campus missions and insist on quality in relation to those missions. This theory undergirds the definition of collegiate quality offered by E. Grady Bogue and Robert L. Saunders in their 1992 book *The Evidence for Quality*: "Quality is conformance to mission specification and goal achievement—within publicly accepted standards of accountability and integrity" (p. 20). A similar view may be found in Diana Green's assertion that "a high quality institution is one that clearly states its mission (or purpose) and is efficient and effective in meeting the goals that it has set itself" (1994, p. 15). The operative phrase for this vision of quality is *diversity with distinction*, which carries the idea that each campus should demonstrate quality within its mission.

The Theory of Value-Added. In contrast to the views of quality as based in reputation and quality of resources, Alexander Astin (1985) offers what he describes as a "talent development" definition of excellence: "The most excellent institutions are, in this view, those that have the greatest impact—add the most values, as economists would say—on the student's knowledge and personal development and on the faculty member's scholarly and pedagogical ability and productivity" (p. 61). There is an appealing simplicity to Astin's definition, with its focus on the question of what difference an institution makes in student knowledge, skill, and attitude.

Searching for a definition of quality in higher education takes us on a complex philosophical journey. We will not find the path any less complex as we examine the systems that have evolved to develop and demonstrate quality in our colleges and universities.

Systems for Quality Assurance

At least four streams of activity may be discerned in contemporary approaches for assuring quality in colleges and universities. Accreditation and program reviews exemplify the more traditional approaches, embracing the principles of peer review and external standards. Another approach is the assessment-and-outcomes movement, which calls for the development of performance evidence and attention to value-added questions. Total Quality Management (TQM) is a third movement in both corporate and collegiate settings; it invites our attention to continuous improvement and customer satisfaction. Finally, many states and countries, and some institutions, are requiring periodic accountability and performance indicator reports.

Traditional Peer Review Evaluations. Higher education has fashioned several approaches to quality assurance that include the following traditional instruments: (1) accreditation: the test of mission and goal achievement; (2) rankings and ratings: the test of reputation; and (3) program reviews: the test of peer evaluation.

A thorough description of the history and philosophical elements of each of these tools and an assessment of their strengths and liabilities may be found in *The Evidence for Quality* (Bogue and Saunders, 1992).

In the United States, the oldest and best known seal of collegiate quality is accreditation. It is built on the premise and the promise of mission integrity and performance improvement. Other countries also have forms of accreditation—such as those in New Zealand (New Zealand Qualifications Authority, 1993) and the Philippines (Cooney and Paqueo-Arreza, 1995). In the Netherlands, accreditation is discipline centered (Palmer, 1995). Central to most accreditation processes is a periodic institutional or program self-study, followed by a visit by an external panel of peers who evaluate the program's or institution's compliance with a set of external standards.

Accreditation in the United States is distinguished by the fact that it is a nongovernmental form of quality assurance. It is an instrument that has had an unquestionably positive impact on the improvement of higher education. Accreditation is under frequent and critical assault, however, for a range of imperfections—it has been called an episodic exercise in professional back-scratching, or an exercise built on minimalist standards whose processes and activities are often hidden from public view. Accreditation is also criticized for failing to prevent problems in both academic and administrative integrity. In addition, in the United States accreditation presents the challenge of reconciling the interests of institutional accreditation by six regional agencies with the interests of disciplinary accrediting associations who conduct program accreditation reviews in many different fields. These criticisms notwithstanding, accreditation remains an important and constructive form of quality assurance.

We cannot readily predict changes that may transpire in accreditation, at least in the United States. One possibility, however, is that institutional accreditation, currently under the auspices of six nongovernmental regional agencies, might be transformed into national—though still nongovernmental—accrediting agencies for different types of institutions, such as research universities, comprehensive universities, liberal arts colleges, two-year technical and community colleges, and so on. Another possibility is that accreditation may take the form of an audit, in which external evaluators periodically examine evidence maintained by the institution that demonstrates compliance with external standards of quality. Audits are being explored in several countries, including England, New Zealand, and Australia.

A second traditional quality assurance instrument is academic program review. Program reviews feature self-study and external peer review at the discipline, department, or program level. Although program reviews are a highly respected instrument of quality assurance in higher education, especially in research universities, they are occasionally viewed by faculty as empty and futile exercises—serving as busywork to occupy some administrators and having little relationship to resource allocation and other decisions. Among works describing the philosophical tenets and processes of program review are Barak (1982) and Barak and Breier (1990).

Ranking and rating studies—including the well-known *U.S. News and World Report* ratings of America's "best" colleges, and contemporary rankings of graduate programs such as the National Research Council's Committee for the Study of Research-Doctorate Programs in the United States (Goldberger, Mailer, and Flattau, 1995)—keep the conversation on quality alive but are indicted for offering little help toward improving programs. They also ignore one of the largest sectors of higher education: two-year technical and community colleges. College rankings have been called "quantified gossip" or "navel gazing."

Although media reports of college rankings may suggest that they aid consumer choice, evidence is lacking that such rankings are used in this way. According to a 1995 report in *Student Poll,* "Rankings such as those in *U.S. News and World Report* and *Money Magazine* have little impact on college choice. They are used less frequently by students and have far less influence than most other sources of information and advice" (1995, p. 1).

Readers interested in a more extended treatment of ranking and rating studies will find helpful background in a chapter on that theme in *The Evidence for Quality* (Bogue and Saunders, 1992) and in two critical reviews of ranking (Webster, 1983; Webster and Skinner, 1996). Clearly, rankings and ratings are built on the limited-supply theory of quality, though most studies of this type also attempt to recognize institutional mission in comparing institutions with similar programs.

The Assessment-and-Outcomes Movement. The assessment movement in higher education, a development primarily of the latter part of the twentieth century, centers on the acquisition of multiple forms of evidence in the evaluation of both student and program performance. Assessment focuses attention on results more than on reputation. The nature of personal and organizational performance is too complex to be captured in a single data point. Just as physicians do not have a holistic health meter in their offices but assess our health by examining a cluster of medical evidence, so we need a cluster of performance assessments and evidence in order to make judgments about quality in students, programs, and institutions. We can, and should, know as much about our students upon their exit as we do upon their entry—about the changes in their knowledge, skills, and attitudes.

Here we should note the growing involvement in assessment of actors and agencies beyond the campus. In the United States, which has a history of strong institutional autonomy for its public colleges and universities, two-thirds of the states had policy mandates by 1990 that required colleges and universities to assess student learning (Ewell, Finney, and Lenth, 1990). In other countries— such as England, New Zealand, the Netherlands, and Spain—there have been government-based quality assurance initiatives. Indeed, the two most obvious policy initiatives in the United States and in many other countries in the latter half of the twentieth century have involved increasing access to higher education and enhancing public accountability for quality.

Whether assessment activities have been linked effectively to teaching and learning or to the improvement of what happens in classrooms, laboratories, and studios remains an open question on many campuses. Too often assessment is undertaken for pro forma and cosmetic purposes of meeting external government mandates. However, the books *Making a Difference* (Banta and Associates, 1994) and *Assessment in Practice* (Banta and others, 1995) furnish a range of institutional illustrations that support the constructive impact of the assessment movement.

Total Quality Management. A more recent system of quality assurance in higher education was originally developed for corporations, especially in the manufacturing industries. Built on the pioneering work of W. Edwards Deming (1986), TQM emphasizes continuous improvement and systems analysis. Daniel Seymour's *On Q: Causing Quality in Higher Education* (1992) provides an informative and integrating treatment of the application of TQM in higher education.

In addition to its focus on the continuous improvement principle, TQM also focuses on the principle of customer satisfaction. Although some academics are uncomfortable with the idea of students as customers, few would argue that we listen enough to our students, and fewer still would assert that we cannot improve our programs and services by seeking evaluations from our students. Indeed, surveys of enrolled students and graduates have been conducted for years (Bogue and Saunders, 1992).

There are, however, critical differences between corporate and collegiate settings regarding the principle of customer satisfaction and the concept of student as customer. Any faculty member who has experienced tension between caring for students and caring for standards knows the limitation of this test for quality in colleges and universities. And it is not an exaggeration to say that it is possible for some students to be highly satisfied yet remain relatively uneducated.

Some faculty and administrative officers see TQM as appropriate for improvements in the admissions office, the business office, the facilities maintenance office, the campus security office, or other administrative settings. Others note, as does Seymour, that these are not the only settings where "we degrade, we hassle, and we ignore" (1992, p. 115). Will we find opportunities for listening to our clients and for problem solving in the academic heart of colleges and universities? Here students can be placed in harm's way by low and empty expectations, by assessment exercises having little or no decision-making utility, by a vision of quality that depends more on the number of faculty publications than on teaching and caring for our students.

Accountability and Performance Indicator Reporting. In addition to the traditional approaches to quality assurance, the emergence of the assessment movement, and the current applications of TQM in college settings, a fourth stream of activity is also discernible: accountability and performance indicator reporting. As noted earlier, it is clear that governments are increasingly interested in the question of quality. In the United States, a 1993 study published by the Southern Regional Education Board indicated that all but two of the fifteen states in the Southern region had either a legislative mandate or another requirement that imposed an annual comprehensive accountability report on public colleges and universities (Bogue, Creech, and Folger, 1993). Other nations are also developing forms of indicator reporting. (See, for example, reports of work in the Netherlands by Segers and Dochy, 1996.)

Among the indicators typically found in accountability reports are enrollment trends, student performance on admissions examinations, retention and graduation rates, pass rates on licensure and other professional examinations, job placement rates, and student and alumni satisfaction. Although a performance indicator may be defined as quantitative data on any aspect of institutional or program performance, some writers prefer to distinguish a performance indicator from a management statistic (Segers and Dochy, 1996). A data point, in this distinction, is a performance indicator if it reflects information or intelligence related to a program or institutional goal, and it is a management statistic if it reflects activity or achievement in an area of management interest that is not directly related to a goal.

A discussion of definitions leads to the question of the purposes served by performance indicator reporting. Performance indicator reports may allow colleges and universities to demonstrate accountability to public bodies, establish trend lines of activity and achievement, and mark progress on goals for higher education. The last purpose is clearly a means for demonstrating stewardship of government resources.

A monograph entitled *Measuring Up: The Promises and Pitfalls of Performance Indicators in Higher Education* states that "higher education has been reluctant to develop performance indicators because it is felt that the mission of higher education is too diverse to measure, and that short-term measurement may not provide adequate measurement of long-term student and scholarship success. However, if the members of the academy—faculty, academic leaders, and students—do not participate in the process of developing and improving the use of performance indicators, external organizations will force some form of indicators on them" (Gaither, Nedwek, and Neal, 1994, pp. x–xi).

Few would argue that the press for accountability reporting and use of performance indicators, or indeed the entire pressure for quality assurance, is without major liabilities. Writing in a special issue of *Change* devoted to the "vexing trend" of accountability reporting, Roger Peters expresses a faculty perspective in noting that "effective assessment requires a diligent search for bad news, which is more useful than good, but accountability encourages the opposite. Campus officials are understandably reluctant to bear bad tidings to those who fund them" (1994, pp. 18–19).

This inclination, of course, is not restricted to collegiate organizations. If one examined the annual report of a business about to enter bankruptcy, it is questionable whether one would find a hint of that probability in the annual report. Some say we tend to construct indicators that reflect the ease of capturing data rather than identify those criteria that will carry valid evidence of performance.

An argument can be made, however, that both institutions and government need performance intelligence on activity and achievement—intelligence that allows decision makers to know something about the health of the enterprise, to establish a basis for making improvements in both instructional and administrative services, and to demonstrate the extent to which progress is being made on public goals. In this sense, a well-conceived profile of performance indicators allows an educational program, an institution, or a system of institutions to offer an operational expression of its quality, to satisfy simultaneously the calls of improvement and accountability, and to enhance its decision capability.

To ensure that systems of quality assurance are integrated and complement one another, to ensure that there is faculty and staff awareness of and allegiance to these systems, and to ensure that data acquired from quality assurance systems are used to improve decisions are notable design challenges. We design climates for learning with our ideals just as surely as with our ideas, however. Thus another design challenge is to cultivate those values that will honor quality in our daily and personal journeys in colleges and universities. Let us turn, then, to this more personal dimension of quality assurance.

Beyond Systems: The Moral and Ethical Dimension of Quality

There is more to quality assurance than systems. Nurturing and assuring quality in colleges and universities is as much a moral activity as it is a technical one, as much personal as it is systemic, in both its content and its tactics. Consider the quality implications of the following acts:

An administrative officer or faculty member defends the educational standards of a college or university against political interference.
A faculty member calls a student to accountability for cheating on a test or plagiarizing a paper.
An academic administrator stands against shallow curricular provisions in an academic program.
A department or program chair holds a faculty member accountable for effective performance.
A state, regional, or national official holds an institution accountable for misrepresentation of the programs it is authorized to offer.

A major state university and its medical school in the United States admitted patients for heart transplant surgery with the full knowledge that probably none of these surgeries would actually take place. Both patients and insurance companies were billed for large sums. Those who were aware of this cruel charade included some medical faculty, the dean of the medical school, and upper-level administrators. A public audit revealed these misdeeds (see also Bogue, 1994). This act was not about duplicity and mismanagement of research, the degradation of academic credentials, or the careless stewardship of public resources. It was a callous disregard for human life and dignity in an academic and professional field whose purposes are to revere and enhance human life and dignity. From this and a hundred other depressing and bizarre stories that have made their way into the public press we may understand more fully why our nonacademic friends may question whether higher education has severed the precious link between mind and heart, whether our pursuit of technical competence is unaccompanied by cultivation of conscience. And we may understand why colleges and universities are no longer viewed as places of sanctuary where values other than the purely financial and selfish might prevail, where commitment to truth and unfettered inquiry nurtures a standard of conduct marked by nobility and integrity (Bogue, 1994).

Thus, the cause of quality can be either advanced or damaged in personal moments in the lives of college administrators and faculty, in a thousand "moments of truth" (Carlzon, 1987) occurring in our colleges and universities every day. Quality assurance, therefore, is a responsibility invested not only in the technical systems that have evolved. Quality assurance is just as surely invested in the minds and hearts, in the values and courage, of the faculty and administrators who hold our climates of learning in trust. Although the metaphor of corporate and collegiate leaders orchestrating organizational behavior and serving as organizational maestros can be viewed as confining, we find it to be an informative metaphor that conveys useful truth. It is possible for an individual musician or a musical ensemble of any size, including a full orchestra, to play correctly—or as the TQM statistical process control folks might say, with zero defects, in control and capable. But in the orchestra hall patrons know that a correct yet dull and uninspired performance is not necessarily quality music. If the music lacks passion and fire, inventiveness and imagination, correctness will not transform it into a quality performance. In the orchestra hall of our college or university will our students not also be able to discern when we are correct—and when we care?

Governing Ideals and Design Principles

It would perhaps be both arrogant and unwise to suggest that "good practice" in quality assurance could be conveniently summarized in a small number of bulleted ideas or principles. For faculty and administrators, board members and government officials, however, who aspire to design effective quality assurance systems, the following questions might at least serve as opening points of discussion:

Can the program or institution offer rich evidence or multiple indicators of both performance and improvement, activity and achievement?
Are these indicators of performance being used to make increasingly informed decisions on policy, program, and personnel?
Is the distinctive mission of the program, institution, or both affirmed and advanced by the indicators of quality and performance selected?

Are quality assurance systems designed to minimize duplication of effort and to maximize usefulness for decisions? Is there an awareness of and allegiance to the overall approach by faculty and staff?

Is each quality assurance instrument clearly linked to teaching and learning and its impact realized?

Is the campus making use of external standards and judgments that go beyond the confines of its own experience and faculty?

Conserving the past, criticizing the present, constructing the future—this is a complex mission that destines colleges and universities to remain always in the crucible of public conversation. It also guarantees a continuing tension between civic expectation and the evaluation of higher education mission and performance. For organizations that are established to honor our social, economic, political, cultural, and scientific heritage even as they criticize that heritage, that hold hands with the past even as they reach for the future, quality assurance is a majestic and complex challenge.

The concepts of providing evidence of performance, of continuous quality improvement and decision utility, of responding to accountability demands by parties external to the campus, and of recognizing mission differences and clarifying them are important governing and design ideals of quality. Designing well-crafted quality assurance systems that embrace these principles, ensuring that these systems are integrated and complementary in function, and taking steps to develop faculty and staff ownership of and allegiance to these systems are conceptual or head-first leadership challenges of the first order.

The nurturing of quality in our colleges and universities, however, must go beyond these conceptual and technical responsibilities. Beyond systems of accreditation and assessment, TQM and accountability reporting, we need faculty and administrators who have a keen sense of standard and right behavior, who answer the call to honor and are willing to use moral outrage as an instrument of quality assurance, who create quality climates via the influence of their ideals as well as their ideas. Thus the critical design elements of collegiate excellence and quality may be the heart-first actions of caring and courage.

What unites the systemic and the personal dimensions of quality assurance? The uniting element is a habit of mind and heart that creates a community of caring. The visibility accorded to institutions that have a substantive and sustained reputation for quality may not come primarily from being models of assessment. Rather, it may come from a community of caring, created over many years, in which the personal and the systemic servants of quality are almost indistinguishable.

In a community of caring, vision and expectation call students and colleagues from the poverty of the commonplace and launch them to the far reaches of their promise. Courage and compassion create a climate in which a respect for diversity of mission and talent is matched with a scorn for shoddy work, whether individual or institutional. Policy and action together translate the call of honor into specific acts essential to the nurture of both students and standards. A community of caring responds not only to the intellectual and institutional call of advancing the truth but also to the ethical and personal call of honoring dignity, justice, and responsibility. In a community of caring, quality does not and cannot live apart from integrity.

References

Astin, A. *Achieving Educational Excellence: A Critical Assessment of Priorities and Practices in Higher Education.* San Francisco: Jossey-Bass, 1985.

Banta, T., and Associates. *Making a Difference.* San Francisco: Jossey-Bass, 1994.

Banta, T., Lund, J., Black, K., and Oblander, F. *Assessment in Practice.* San Francisco: Jossey-Bass, 1995.

Barak, R. *Program Review in Higher Education.* Boulder, Colo.: National Center for Higher Education Management Systems, 1982.

Barak, R., and Breier, B. *Successful Program Review: A Practical Guide to Evaluating Programs in Academic Settings.* San Francisco: Jossey-Bass, 1990.

Bogue, E. *Leadership by Design: Strengthening Integrity in Higher Education.* San Francisco: Jossey-Bass, 1994.

Bogue, E., Creech, J., and Folger, J. *Assessing Quality in Higher Education: Policy Actions in SREB States.* Atlanta, Ga.: Southern Regional Education Board, 1993.

Bogue, E., and Saunders, R. *The Evidence for Quality.* San Francisco: Jossey-Bass, 1992.

Carlzon, J. *Moments of Truth.* Cambridge, Mass: Ballinger, 1987.

Cartter, A. *An Assessment of Quality in Graduate Education.* Washington, D.C.: American Council on Education, 1964.

Crosby, P. *Quality Without Tears.* New York: McGraw-Hill, 1984.

Cooney, R. and Paqueo-Arreza, E. "Higher Education Regulation in the Phillippines: Issues of Control, Quality Assurance, and Accreditation." In A. Yee (ed.), *East Asian Higher Education.* Oxford, England: Pergamon Press, 1995.

Deming, W. *Out of the Crisis.* Cambridge, Mass.: MIT Press, 1986.

Ewell, P., Finney, J., and Lenth, C. "Filling in the Mosaic: The Emerging Pattern of State-Based Assessment." *AAHE Bulletin,* 1990, 42 (8), 3–5.

Gaither, G., Nedwek, B., and Neal, J. *Measuring Up: The Promises and Pitfalls of Performance Indicators in Higher Education.* ASHE-ERIC Higher Education Report 94-5. Washington, D.C.: School of Education and Human Services, George Washington University, 1994.

Garvin, D. *Managing Quality.* New York: Free Press, 1988.

Goldberger, M., Maher, B., and Flattau, P. (eds.). *Research Doctorate Programs in the United States: Continuity and Change.* Washington, D.C.: National Academy Press, 1995.

Green, D. *What Is Quality in Higher Education?* London: The Society for Research into Higher Education/Open University Press, 1994.

Guaspari, J. *I Know When I See It: A Modern Fable About Quality.* New York: AMACOM, 1985.

New Zealand Qualifications Authority. *The Approval and Accreditation of Degrees and Related Qualifications: Quality Assurance in Education and Training.* Wellington: New Zealand Qualifications Authority, 1993.

Palmer, B. "Lesjes van de Nederlanders: Little Lessons from the Dutch to Promote Educational Quality." Paper presented at the Association for Institutional Research thirty-fourth annual Forum Place, Boston, May 1995.

Peters, R. "Some Sharks Are Boojum: Accountability and the Ethos of Higher Education." *Change,* 1994, 26 (6), 16–23.

Segers, M., and Dochy, F. "Quality Assurance in Higher Education: Theoretical Considerations and Empirical Studies." *Studies in Educational Evaluation,* 1996, 22 (2), 115–137.

Seymour, D. *On Q: Causing Quality in Higher Education.* Phoenix: Oryx Press, 1992.

Student Poll, 1995, 1 (1).

Webster, D. "America's Highest Ranked Graduate Schools, 1925–1982." *Change,* 1983, *15* (4), 14–24.

Webster, D., and Skinner, T. "Rating Ph.D. Programs: What the NRC Report Says . . . and Doesn't Say." *Change,* 1996, *28* (3), 22–50.

Wilson, L. "Foreword." In A. Cartter (ed.), *An Assessment of Quality in Graduate Education.* Washington, D.C.: American Council on Education, 1964.

E. GRADY BOGUE *is professor in the Department of Education Leadership at the University of Tennessee and chancellor emeritus of Louisiana State University in Shreveport.*

The Dutch quality improvement model has successfully maintained a delicate balance between internal improvement and external accountability, but the faculty's clear ownership of the system—as opposed to the government's ownership in other nations—has made continuous quality improvement a dominant feature of the current Dutch system.

Quality Assurance in the Netherlands

Peter A. M. Maassen

During the 1970s and 1980s many European higher education systems were confronted with a number of far-reaching changes in their environments. Most of these changes can be related to a shift in the increased demand for education and the altered relationship between government and higher education. A major underlying force causing this shift was the rise to power of conservative governments throughout Europe. The governmental "value-for-money" approach led to the end of the unconditional public funding of higher education. In practice this implied, among other things, that the funding of higher education was increasingly linked to the performance of universities and colleges. As a consequence, the issue of how to assess the quality of the activities of higher education institutions became very important. Because hardly any nation in Europe had the kind of formal quality assessment experiences desired, many of those involved in the change processes became interested in the practices of quality assessment used elsewhere, especially in North American higher education.

Even though the North American experiences were very helpful in the early period of this change, it soon became clear that the specific European national contexts required a different approach to quality assessment. This need was mainly the result of the dominant coordinating position of the central governments in Europe, which wanted to use information on institutional performance for their own purposes (Clark, 1983). This situation implied that a quality assurance practice had to be developed that could be used by both institutions and governments.

The Netherlands, France, and Great Britain were the first countries in Europe where the contours of a new formal quality assessment system became visible in the mid-1980s (Maassen, 1997). For both sectors of the Dutch binary higher education system—that is, the university and the higher professional education (or college) sectors—an approach was developed based on self-evaluation followed by peer review through visiting committees (see Figure 2.1). In both sectors the unit to be evaluated was not the institution as a whole but the study program. Performance indicators have not been used, although they were strongly advocated by the government from the beginning.

Even though the interest in quality was not a new phenomenon in Dutch higher education in the 1980s (Neave, 1994), the way in which the quality of higher education was ensured at that time was apparently not sufficiently effective enough in the eyes of the government. In 1985 a governmental policy paper called *HOAK* (Dutch abbreviation for *Higher Education: Autonomy and Quality*; Ministry of Education and Science, 1985) was published that explained the intended new coordination relationship between government and higher education. The universities and colleges would become more autonomous if they would cooperate in the development of a comprehensive quality assurance system in which all aspects of the performance of higher education institutions would be assessed regularly. This system of quality assurance incorporated a drift toward a more market-oriented higher education system. As one of the suggested outcomes of this development, universities and colleges were expected to develop a kind of strategic behavior leading to clearly distinguishable institutional profiles. These profiles were to be based on increased knowledge of the institution's performance.

Figure 2.1. The Quality Assurance Cycle in Dutch Higher Education

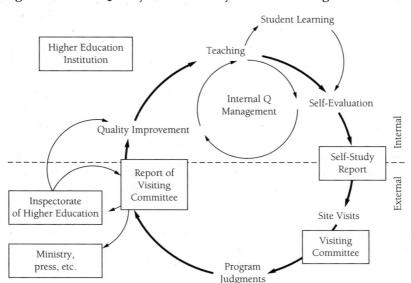

Source: Adapted from Westerheijden, 1997b.

The changes did not imply that the government completely devolved its responsibilities for higher education. The Dutch minister of education and science made it clear during the discussions of a new bill for higher education in 1992 that governmental responsibility was not supposed to fade away. Rather, an appropriate description for the new higher education coordination approach would be a selectively involved government—the government would be present but it would choose its particular points of involvement. In addition, the bilateral consultative structure between the government and higher education institutions for the development and implementation of higher education policies was opened to include external stakeholders, such as employers of higher education graduates as well as local and regional politicians. The latter development was linked to the governmental attempt to stimulate Dutch institutions to develop managerial modes of operation and businesslike behavior, as also happened with universities and colleges in other European countries (see, for example, Larsen and Gornitzka, 1995).

The combination of the collegial and political model of decision making that formed the basis for the university as an organization until the 1970s has been replaced by so-called entrepreneurial management (Neave and Van Vught, 1991; Clark, 1998). The most important characteristics of entrepreneurial management are

Increased involvement of external constituencies in central institutional decision making

More emphasis on developing and implementing institutional strategies

More interest in the application of management techniques developed in the corporate world

All in all, the political context of the Dutch higher education system has changed drastically over the last ten to fifteen years, with the introduction of formal quality assurance mechanisms in higher education being one of the most important results.

Guiding Principles, Purposes, and Objectives

The guiding principle for the development of the quality assurance system for Dutch higher education after 1985 was that in exchange for a greater degree of financial and managerial autonomy the higher education institutions would demonstrate that they deliver quality education. Originally the government intended this evaluation to be executed by the Inspectorate for Higher Education (IHO). Through subsequent negotiations in 1986 a compromise was reached that would involve the representative organizations of the higher education institutions—the Association of Cooperating Universities in the Netherlands (abbreviated VSNU in Dutch) for the universities, and the HBO-Council for the higher professional education institutions—in the quality assurance process. This meant that in practice two separate quality assurance systems were developed, one for the universities coordinated by the VSNU and one for the higher professional education sector, coordinated by the HBO-Council. Through that compromise the IHO was bypassed and was largely left with the task of meta-evaluation: evaluation of the evaluations and evaluation of the follow-up on the assessment results obtained by the higher education institutions.

Both the VSNU and the HBO-Council emphasized that the quality assurance systems they were developing should serve two purposes: quality improvement and accountability (Vroeijenstijn and Acherman, 1990; Westerheijden, 1997b). Quality improvement refers to the internal functions of the quality assurance process. The process should allow the institutions to use the self-evaluations and peer reviews to improve the quality of teaching as well as the organization of the teaching program. This is done through formative evaluations, such as recommendations on how improvements can be realized (Kells, 1995). Accountability emphasizes the external functions of quality assurance. It refers to the governmental expectation that public money be spent in an acceptable and satisfying way in higher education. Accountability evaluations are summative, that is, they provide data on the quality of specific aspects of the teaching process, such as dropout and time-to-degree ratios.

In the university sector, a first pilot project was coordinated by the VSNU in 1988. As a result of this pilot project, some adjustments were made and the quality assessment procedure became operational in 1989. In 1990 the HBO-Council started a procedure in the higher professional education sector that, although not identical to the VSNU approach, was based on the same principles. One of these main underlying principles was the separation of the evaluation of teaching from the evaluation of research. A formal system of quality assessment for research had already existed in the Netherlands since 1982. It was part of a separate funding mechanism for university research. Research evaluations were included in the teaching assessment insofar as they were important for the teaching process or its environment (quality of staff and so forth). In both sectors, all study programs have subsequently been evaluated in the first cycles (six years for all universities and seven years for professional education programs). On the basis of the results and experiences in the first cycle, the procedures will be adapted for the second cycle.

The Process

The cycle and process span two distinct educational arenas, and the boundaries of each application are well defined. Therefore, we begin by discussing the university sector and then in a separate section present specifics concerning the process in the higher professional education sector.

The University Sector. The VSNU used U.S. and Canadian experiences with program review and specialized accreditation to develop its own system, which is collectively owned (and funded) by the universities. The system has led to a change in emphasis in the aims of quality assurance: from a predominant emphasis on accountability to a primary emphasis on quality improvement. The focal point of the VSNU quality assurance procedure is the visiting committee that reviews all study programs in a specific subject area (see Figure 2.1). A study program is interpreted as a collection of courses leading to the first degree—a degree equivalent to a master's degree in the United States. The approach focuses on disciplinary fields instead of on institutions as a whole. In principle, in a six-year cycle all study programs are assessed.

In preparation for the visiting committee, each study program is required to write a self-evaluation. The aims of the self-evaluation are not only to prepare the faculty for the visiting committee but also to stimulate internal quality management (Vroeijenstijn and Acherman, 1990). The content of the self-evaluation is not completely fixed; prior to the evaluation of their programs the faculties and departments can stress points that are important to them. For reasons of comparability, however, a guideline is given by the VSNU in the form of a checklist (Vroeijenstijn, 1994). The checklist consists of a large number of topics to be addressed in the self-evaluation, such as program goals, the organization of the program, student and staff information, and data on graduates. It is a list of factual data needed, not a list of performance indicators; it is neither quantitative nor qualitative, though some data might be interpreted in that way. It also is not a list of minimum requirements. The study program's own goals are the point of departure. The list includes data on the academic staff and its quality, but no specific data are required on research output or quality, or on how research and teaching are related. The self-evaluations of each participating study program are collected by the visiting committee before it visits the program.

Each visiting committee consists of about seven members, including at least one foreign expert in the field (with knowledge of the Dutch language and the Dutch higher education system) and one educational expert. The other members preferably are chosen from outside any involved program, and an even distribution over the several subspecialisms is sought. In practice, special care is taken to appoint an independent chair. The members of the committee are proposed by the collective deans of the participating faculties and nominated by the board of the VSNU.

Normally a committee visits each study program for two or two and a half days. During this period the committee speaks with representatives of all interest groups involved in the program, including students. Subjects for the talks are based on the self-evaluation, the committee's prior visits and other knowledge of the field, the topics proposed by the faculty or department responsible for the study program, and anything else that comes up during the visit. At the end of the visit, the chair gives an oral, temporary statement about the quality of the study program. On the basis of the written version of this statement, and on the basis of the (factual) comments provided by the staff of the study programs, the visiting committee then writes its final report. The report usually contains a statement of general problems, outlooks, expectations, and recommendations pertaining to the field, as well as chapters about each individual study program.

The Higher Professional Education Sector. The institutions for higher professional education use the same general principles as the universities do in their evaluations of teaching programs (see Figure 2.1). The HBO-Council started its coordinating role in 1990. Because of the large number of teaching programs in this sector, the quality assurance system operates on a seven-year cycle. In subject areas that have many study programs, two or more external committees share the burden of visiting and reviewing the programs.

The main differences between these evaluations and those of universities are a result of the strong vocational focus of the study programs in the professional education sector. Consequently, the applicability of knowledge and job orientation have a higher priority in the professional education sector than in the university sector. The HBO-Council has therefore developed its own guidelines for self-evaluation that differ in a number of respects from the guidelines used by the VSNU for the university programs. Although these guidelines are used by the institutional units for their self-evaluations, the visiting committee is free to work out its own concept of quality.

The HBO-Council begins with the notion that a uniform assessment framework is impossible because the teaching programs in this sector differ too much in many aspects relative to the specific professional fields for which they train their students. Nonetheless, to prevent arbitrariness, a visiting committee's assessment framework has to fulfill three conditions (Van Hartingsveld, 1994). First, the assessment framework must be included explicitly in the final report. Those being evaluated have the right to know through which framework their teaching program has been reviewed. Second, the assessment framework must be worked out and explained clearly. This means that at the minimum the following must be included in a committee's report: a definition of quality, the evaluation questions used to examine quality as it has been defined by the committee, the substantive aspects of a teaching program and the organization on which the review has focused, and the standards used to judge the quality of these aspects and organizational variables. Finally, the assessment framework must be constructed in a way that allows the committee to justify its choices, recommendations, and conclusions in an open, convincing, and valid way.

The HBO-Council has produced a handbook to support the visiting committees. The handbook discusses six different perspectives on the concept of quality: the formal/legal, the subject/discipline, the business economics, the consumer, the market, and the organizational innovation perspectives. Each perspective focuses on quality from a different angle, and in doing so highlights a specific point of view of the primary function of a higher education institution. By providing these different perspectives, the HBO-Council limits the range of the visiting committee's choices in decisions made within its assessment framework. The composition of the visiting committees is different from the composition of university committees. Whereas the latter consist of academic peers, the HBO-Council uses mainly experienced external practitioners from the professional field on which the study program is focused.

Results

An important aspect of the Dutch quality assurance system is that the outcomes of the evaluations are not used directly by the government for policy or funding purposes. As a result of the agreements of 1986, the Ministry of Education and Science does not take any action on the basis of the visiting committees' judgments. It assumes that the assessment system should not be hampered by potential direct consequences for decision making and funding. Direct links to funding and other aspects of government decision making can be expected to lead too easily to strategic behavior on the part of the higher education institutions that will undermine completely the quality assessment system. A way has thereby been found to escape what may be called "the dilemma of quality assessment": "Without the expectation of real consequences, the incentives to organize quality assessment are lacking; with the expectation of real consequences, quality assessment will turn into a power game" (Westerheijden, 1990, p. 206). The Ministry of Education and Science has found its way out of this dilemma by abstaining from direct intervention but simultaneously making it known that it may take action in the medium or long term. To make sure that quality assurance is taken seriously in the absence of a direct threat, the IHO, on behalf of the Ministry of Education and Science, is responsible for the so-called meta-evaluation of the system. Consequently, the IHO examines regularly the peer review reports of the visiting committees and the extent to which the institutions have used the outcomes of the internal and external evaluations.

The first task of the IHO is to verify whether the visiting committee worked according to the established procedure—that is, whether the conclusions and recommendations reached by each committee were based on valid information. Since the start of the first six-year evaluation cycle at the end of the 1980s, only one university visiting committee's report has been rejected. This meant that the external peer review process had to be repeated. Likewise, in the higher professional education sector only one external report has not been accepted.

Since 1993 the IHO has assumed a second task. It investigates how the institutions react to the recommendations and conclusions of the visiting committees. Institutions have to produce an action plan after a unit is evaluated, specifying their follow-up to the evaluation. If the action plan is unsatisfactory, the minister of education will issue a so-called yellow card—a warning that an institution has to improve the teaching program of the evaluated unit in a serious way or the funding of the program will be stopped. Such a warning is also given when one or more parts of a study program are considered to be very weak. In such a case the institution is asked to make rapid improvements. Until now only one warning has been given in the university sector and only a few in the higher professional education sector. Apparently the threat of receiving a yellow card stimulates the institutions sufficiently to induce the expected improvements.

The final task of the IHO is self-imposed. The IHO checks what has happened in response to the evaluations three years after the publication of the visiting committee's report, to make sure that the action plans have been implemented. All in all the IHO's meta-evaluation suggests that the quality assurance system works reasonably well, both in the universities and in the higher professional education institutions. This conclusion has been confirmed by a number of independent research projects on the effects of the quality evaluations. These projects indicate that only a small proportion of the evaluated units do not use the outcomes of the evaluations at all (Frederiks, Westerheijden, and Weusthof, 1994).

Compared to the situation before 1985, the interest in and attention to quality assurance in both types of Dutch higher education institutions has increased significantly (Weusthof, 1995). This does not mean that all institutions implement all the recommendations of the visiting committees. Frederiks (1996) has estimated that about 50 percent of the recommendations are followed. Still, in most cases where institutional units rejected the recommendations, they did so on the basis of clear arguments. So far faculties and departments in universities and colleges have taken seriously the recommendations and conclusions of the visiting committees concerning their programs. Yet despite the relative satisfaction with the system, adaptations are likely in the years to come. For example, as a result of the growing Europeanization of higher education in the member states of the European Union there is a tendency to organize quality assurance on a more international basis. This will have consequences especially for teaching programs focused on a specific profession such as engineering and medicine. Already the HBO-Council has come up with proposals for the development of an accreditation-like approach to replace the current peer review system. Even though it is too early to conclude anything definitive about the outlook of quality assurance in Dutch higher education in the coming decade, the growing influence of the European context will likely affect Dutch institutions by making them more internationally oriented in the way they try to assure the quality of their activities.

The Balance of Functions in Dutch Quality Assurance

The Dutch experience offers an interesting balance between the internal improvement and the external accountability functions of quality assurance. Because of the institutions' ownership of the system of quality assurance, they have been able to emphasize the improvement function, although the government can also force the institutions to take the accountability function seriously through IHO's meta-evaluation of the system. The emphasis on improvement is apparent when the Dutch system is compared to other European quality assurance approaches (Van Vught and Westerheijden, 1993). The British approach provides an especially interesting contrast because their quality assurance mechanisms, until recently, seem to be mainly oriented toward accountability and therefore of limited effectiveness (Harvey and Knight, 1996). The internal improvement orientation in Dutch higher education is supported by involving the program's academic staff in the evaluation processes. The meta-evaluation of the IHO and the research in this area support this assertion. This support is important because of the power of the academic staff in enhancing improvement and reform or providing resistance. It can be argued that the implementation of any of the outcomes of the evaluations is dependent on their cooperation (Maassen, 1996). Only if the faculty accept the legitimacy of the improvement function of the quality assurance system can the institutional administrators as well as the academic staff use the results. Research on the effects of quality assurance (see, for example, Westerheijden, 1997a) has shown that institutional administrators believe that this legitimization might be the most important aspect of the quality assurance systems developed and implemented since the end of the 1980s. Until then administrators knew about good and bad teaching activities and other aspects of higher education, but they could not use this knowledge for decisions because they lacked the support of the faculty, who often repudiated or resisted the administrators' judgments on the basis of their source or legitimacy. The external part of the quality assurance mechanism (see Figure 2.1) provided the needed legitimacy through the reliance on peer judgment.

The Dutch quality assurance process in higher education offers an interesting model that other countries can consider because it creates legitimacy for using quality-oriented judgments in internal decision-making processes. Even though the Dutch model resulted from governmental initiatives and pressures for accountability, it provides an interesting positive example because Dutch institutions have been able to accommodate the government's desire for accountability to their own needs for internal institutional improvement.

References

Clark, B. R. *The Higher Education System: Academic Organization in Cross-National Perspective.* Berkeley: University of California Press, 1983.

Clark, B. R. *Creating Entrepreneurial Universities: Organizational Pathways of Transformation.* Oxford: Pergamon Press, 1998.

Frederiks, M.M.H. *Beslissen Over Kwaliteit.* Utrecht, the Netherlands: De Tijdstroom, 1996.

Frederiks, M.M.H., Westerheijden, D. F., and Weusthof, P.J.M. "Effects of Quality Assessment in Dutch Higher Education." *European Journal of Education,* 1994, *29,* 181–200.

Harvey, L., and Knight, P. T. *Transforming Higher Education.* Buckingham, England: SRHE/Open University Press, 1996.

Kells, H. R. *Self-Study Processes: A Guide to Self-Evaluation in Higher Education.* (4th ed.) Phoenix: Oryx Press, 1995.

Larsen, I. M., and Gornitzka, Å. "New Management Systems in Norwegian Universities: The Interface Between Reform and Institutional Understanding." *European Journal of Education,* 1995, *30,* 347–361.

Maassen, P.A.M. *Governmental Steering and the Academic Culture. The Intangibility of the Human Factor in Dutch and German Universities.* Utrecht, the Netherlands: De Tijdstroom, 1996.

Maassen, P.A.M. "Quality in European Higher Education: Recent Trends and Their Historical Roots." *European Journal of Education,* 1997, *32,* 111–129.

Ministry of Education and Science. *Hoger Onderwijs: Autonomie en Kwaliteit* [Higher Education: Autonomy and Quality]. The Netherlands: Ministry of Education and Science, 1985.

Neave, G. "The Politics of Quality: Developments in Higher Education in Western Europe, 1992–1994." *European Journal of Education,* 1994, *29,* 115–134.

Neave, G., and Van Vught, F. A. *Prometheus Bound: The Changing Relationship Between Government and Higher Education in Western Europe.* Oxford, England: Pergamon Press, 1991.

Van Hartingsveld, L. M. "Looking Inside the Black Box. Aspects of Quality Assessment in Higher Vocational Education in the Netherlands." In D. F. Westerheijden, J. Brennan, and P.A.M. Maassen (eds.), *Changing Contexts of Quality Assessment: Recent Trends in West European Higher Education.* Utrecht, the Netherlands: Lemma, 1994.

Van Vught, F. A., and Westerheijden, D. F. *Quality Management and Quality Assurance in European Higher Education: Methods and Mechanisms.* Luxembourg: Office for Official Publications of the European Community, 1993.

Vroeijenstijn, A. I. *Improvement and Accountability: Navigating Between Scylla and Charybdis: Guide for External Quality Assessment in Higher Education.* London: Jessica Kingsley, 1994.

Vroeijenstijn, A. I., and Acherman, J. A. "Control Oriented Versus Improvement Oriented Quality Assessment." In L. Goedegebuure, P. Maassen, and D. Westerheijden (eds.), *Peer Review and Performance Indicators: Quality Assessment in British and Dutch Higher Education.* Utrecht, the Netherlands: Lemma, 1990.

Westerheijden, D. F. "Peers, Performance and Power." In L. Goedegebuure, P. Maassen, and D. Westerheijden (eds.), *Peer Review and Performance Indicators: Quality Assessment in British and Dutch Higher Education.* Utrecht, the Netherlands: Lemma, 1990.

Westerheijden, D. F. "A Solid Base for Decisions: Use of the VSNU Research Evaluations in Dutch Universities." *Higher Education,* 1997a, *33,* 397–413.

Westerheijden, D. F. "Quality Assessment in Dutch Higher Education: Balancing Improvement and Accountability." *European Journal for Education Law and Policy,* 1997b, *1,* 81–90.

Weusthof, P.J.M. "Internal Quality Assurance in Dutch Universities: Empirical Analysis of Characteristics and Results of Self-Evaluation." *Quality in Higher Education,* 1995, *1,* 235–248.

PETER A. M. MAASSEN *is director of the Center for Higher Education Policy Studies at the University of Twente in the Netherlands.*

Systematic quality assurance in Spanish universities is a recent development, but it is rich in dynamic, fruitful experiences and promise. This chapter describes how Spanish universities are now incorporating and carrying out these new programs, and how these programs are becoming an integral part of the daily functioning of these institutions.

Introducing Quality Assurance in the Spanish University

José-Ginés Mora, Javier Vidal

To understand the current quality assurance movement in Spain, it is necessary to review the recent history of the country's universities. Spanish universities, the oldest of which were founded in the Middle Ages, remained quite stable until the eighteenth century under the influence of the Catholic Church. At the beginning of the nineteenth century, liberalism stemming from the French Revolution changed the structure of the state. The new liberal state was the shield of all citizens against the aristocratic and ecclesiastical oligarchy in the ancient regime. This change brought "(though not without fierce resistance and periods of reaction) the concept of the university as an institution of the state, which now succeeded to the monopoly once wielded by the church in this field" (García-Garrido, 1992, p. 664). Thus in Spain as in other European countries the state monopoly over higher education originated as a mechanism to protect universities against the social sectors that opposed academic freedom and independence of knowledge. The state then became both the guarantor of freedom of teaching and the administrator of universities. This development set the evolution of higher education in Spain (and other continental European countries) apart from the evolution of higher education in other countries, such as the United States, where private ownership of the first colleges provided the guarantee of freedom and independence from such external powers as the state or other forces.

In the Napoleonic system of higher education, the universities were in fact state agencies completely regulated by laws and norms that emanated from the state. Everything in the daily functioning of a higher education institution was a consequence of the application of an external rule that applied to all educational institutions. Until very recently in Spain, academic programs were identical among institutions, with the same curricula and no differences even in the syllabi. Universities had no specific budgets, and expenditures were regulated by the state to the most minute detail. Professors were appointed after a strict selection procedure to be members of a national body of civil servants. They moved frequently from one university to another.

In this stifling atmosphere of state regulation, quality assurance, as currently understood, did not have a place. The higher education processes, from the financial issues to the number of teaching hours of a course, followed established state rules, and deviations from these rules were not permitted, at least in theory. The control of the processes was exclusively *ex-ante* (predicated on what was intended or desired), and criteria and standards were preestablished. The system relied on the integrity of appointed "professor-officials" to assure the strict fulfillment of the rules. Only in cases of glaring misbehavior did the state make an *ex-post* (after-the-fact) intervention to correct the problems.

This extremely regulated higher education system was also an elitist system whose main goal was to prepare the ruling group of the modern state, especially the civil servants. Spanish universities, like their French and Italian counterparts, had a strong professional orientation. The teaching process was focused on the transmission of skills essential to the development of the professions, many of which were in the state structure. The strict system used in the selection of civil servants functioned as an *ex-post* system of quality control. The same function was exerted indirectly by professional associations in other cases (concerning quality matters related to the specific profession) throughout the country.

The situation just described began to change during the 1970s, when the system started to shift from an elite system to mass higher education. Legal changes also helped trigger a complete renovation of the higher education system. The University Reform Act of 1983 formed the basis for the process of emancipation of higher education from the control of the state, as in other European countries in the 1980s (Neave and van Vught, 1991). The main changes introduced by this act were as follows:

Universities became autonomous entities with the capacity to establish their own programs and curricula.
Institutions were conceived as independent and competitive units.
Professors were no longer a national body and began to "belong" to each university.
Responsibility for universities was transferred to the regional governments.
Institutions began to receive public appropriations as a lump sum, and to have wide-ranging capabilities in allocating their funds internally.

There was not only a shift of formal control from the government to the institutions, as in other countries (Woodhouse, 1996), but also a movement from the national government to the regional governments.

These legal changes over the past few decades mean that the state now has less direct control over universities and that higher education has grown, diversified, and regionalized. Besides, the number of universities, the number of students, and the resources committed to higher education have grown substantially (Mora, 1996, 1997b; Mora and Villarreal, 1996).

Spanish universities, then, are currently in a position that could be considered promising and progressive. Nevertheless, it is the general consensus in the academic and governmental sectors that an additional effort must now be made to improve the overall quality of the institutions and their programs. If during the last few years a considerable effort has been made in the growth of higher education, quality improvement is clearly the main goal for the near future. Quality assessment and quality assurance have become central issues in the higher education agenda and in the policies of regional governments.

First Experiences in Quality Assessment

During the 1990s, a comprehensive set of activities has been carried out with the goal of introducing quality assurance in Spanish universities. Many of these efforts are still in the experimental stage, and not all of them have developed as desired. Nevertheless, they represent a dynamic situation in which many enthusiastic people are experimenting with innovative mechanisms to incorporate quality assurance as a systematic tool for improving quality in Spanish universities. This experience of introducing quality assurance procedures should not be considered a theoretical model, but it does serve as a viable example of how quality assurance practices could be introduced widely in a short time.

Accountability of Individual Performance. The traditional Spanish higher education system, monopolized and completely regulated by the state, obviously was not concerned with accountability. As the system became more autonomous and decentralized, however, greater accountability became necessary. Research efforts were first evaluated in 1986 as a prerequisite step to receiving special funds for university projects. Generalized assessment of individuals and institutions did not begin, however, until the early 1990s.

Since 1990, the research and teaching of tenured professors are assessed periodically (research is assessed every six years and teaching, every five). For each positive assessment during the assessment period, professors receive a permanent increase in salary. Each university is in charge of evaluating the teaching quality of its professors. Because of the lack of valid and reliable standards for the assessment of teaching, almost everyone receives a positive assessment. This flawed system had become a way of rewarding seniority, with no significant effects on improving quality.

Many universities have now introduced systematic surveys of students' opinions about the quality of their instruction. The use of these surveys is a controversial issue, although some universities are using the results, particularly when a professor's ratings are remarkably below the average. Such individuals are compelled to receive some pedagogical training. A systematic low rating could also be a reason for denying promotion in some universities. Although these surveys still have many methodological problems, such as validity and reliability, they have had a positive, indirect effect on the quality of institutions.

The responsiveness of teachers to students, for example, has increased considerably, and the fulfillment of teaching duties, tutorials, and other pedagogical activities is higher in institutions that use systematic student surveys.

A national committee composed of experts from different scientific fields is in charge of assessing the research activities of professors. The criteria for assessing research are stricter than those for assessing teaching. Therefore a significant proportion of professors are evaluated negatively in this area. The increase in salary for each positively evaluated research period is not substantial, but these premiums are becoming the key for promotion in the universities.

Although the systematic evaluation of professors in both teaching and research can be regarded as positive, the fact that it is only rigorous or discriminatory enough to produce concrete results in the case of research assessment has introduced the conventional bias of considering research to be more important than teaching in the academic career. This phenomenon is frequent in most higher education systems (Vidal, 1997).

First Institutional Quality Assessment Experiences. The University Reform Act, which devolved autonomy to universities, made a general statement about the necessity of incorporating a formal system of quality assessment in universities. Nevertheless, several years passed before institutions began implementing this principle. In the early 1990s, several studies analyzed the experiences of quality assessment in other countries. At that time, three main models were employed in Europe: the Dutch, the British, and the French. The Dutch model was a translation of American accreditation procedures into the Dutch reality. It was primarily program centered and based on self-studies and external visits (Vroeijenstijn, 1995). Experts recommended this approach for Spain, with institutional assessment of research and management added to teacher evaluation.

The Experimental Program. The Experimental Program for Evaluation of the Quality in the University System, which incorporated the elements of the Dutch approach, was launched in 1993. It evaluated teaching, research, and institutional management in several universities (García, Mora, Pérez, and Rodríguez, 1995; Mora, 1997a). The primary purpose of this experimental project was to try various methods and make proposals for changes based on experience in the experiment. The experiment proved to be extensive enough to draw meaningful conclusions. In general, the Experimental Program attained its main objectives: to test the accuracy of a methodology and to extend the culture of evaluation in Spanish universities. Conversely, some weak points were discovered, such as lack of institutional data for quality assessment, lack of support from leaders in some universities, and some methodological problems as a consequence of the inexperience of the assessors. Generally speaking, in a very short time the project created and extended quality assessment in universities as a first step in improving institutional quality.

The European Project. Immediately after completing the Experimental Program, the European Union launched the European Pilot Project for Evaluating Quality in Higher Education. This too was a pilot project for testing a common methodology among European universities. The methodology was very similar to the one used in the Experimental Program. The European Project permitted modification in the methodology and adapted it to a broader European context. The most important result of that project, however, was the proposal by the European Commission to establish a relatively common system of quality assessment in European universities. This system would be based on the methodology of self-study and external visits, although each country could reorganize the process, keeping any idiosyncratic national characteristics. This European proposal had an important impact in Spain by convincing some skeptical people, especially politicians from central and regional governments, to support quality assessment in universities.

Conclusions from Pilot Assessment Experiences

After this short but intensive experience, several points became clear to persons involved in the process:

Universities should control the quality assessment effort, but some kind of agreement and cooperation with governments should be reached, especially in relation to the consequences of evaluation.
The basic methodology employed (self-study, external visits, and a final report) was adequate.
Research and management should be evaluated employing similar processes.
It is important to overcome the reluctance that some people have toward assessment—and to have the support of the university leaders for the project.
The results of the process should include both internal and external consequences.

Although the main consequence of the assessment process must be the improvement of quality, universities and units should be provided with some kind of incentive to participate and implement the recommendations. The performance funding found in many American states (Layzell, 1998) and in some European countries (Hölttä, 1998) are examples of such an incentive.

The Program for Institutional Evaluation of Quality in Universities

In 1995 the Council of Universities (a national organization composed of representatives of the regional and national governments and the rectors of all universities) approved the Program for Institutional Evaluation of Quality in Universities, hereafter referred to as the Evaluation Program (Consejo de Universidades, 1995). The Evaluation Program formally institutionalized quality assessment in Spanish universities, as an extended and continuous process for the entire university system.

Objectives. The stated objectives of the Evaluation Program are four: to promote quality processes in Spanish universities; to provide to universities methodological tools for the assessment process that would be homogeneous throughout the country and similar to processes used elsewhere in Europe; to provide society, especially students, with relevant and reliable information about the quality of the institutions, their programs, services, and scientific levels; and to provide accountability to the regional governments.

Organizational Structure. The Evaluation Program is headed by the Council of Universities. A technical committee composed of the council's officials and experts in evaluation is in charge of the process. The Evaluation Program evaluates teaching (in programs), research (in the departments related to programs assessed in teaching), and management (in services also related to the programs).

The initial duration of the Evaluation Program is five years. Although the program is not compulsory, almost all universities participated in its first year. The universities that had been involved in the previous pilot projects started at higher participation levels, with an extensive assessment of programs. Universities without such experience started with a prudent, more basic level of participation.

Methodology. The methodology used is the same as that used in some earlier efforts in Spain and recommended by the European Commission. The first step of the process is a self-study carried out by the evaluation committee of each university. The report of this study has two purposes: to promote reliable information on the evaluated unit and to promote awareness of quality issues in the university community. The second step is a visit by an external committee composed of academic and nonacademic experts in the field. They interview leaders, staff, and students in each evaluated unit and compare their findings to the self-study report. This external committee sends a report to the Council of Universities following each visit. In the third step the university issues a published report that synthesizes the self-study and the external committee's report. A general report on the program's first-year activities was recently published (Consejo de Universidades, 1998).

The technical committee has prepared written guidelines to standardize the process in participating universities. These guidelines define criteria and procedures and establish the main points to be assessed and summarized in the committee reports. Nevertheless, the reports had the option to use a different structure. Some universities with more refined internal quality procedures have used the criteria provided by the European Foundation for Quality Management (EFQM) for their self-report. EFQM criteria are based on the application of Total Quality Management (TQM) principles to educational institutions.

Criteria for the Structure of the Reports. All of the reports must use reliable data but must also focus on the analysis, opinions, and judgments of the people involved in the evaluated units. The reports are required to contain recommendations for improvement. They should include the following sections: description and context of units evaluated; information on aims and objectives; information on resources, structure, and results; judgments by the evaluation committee about the strong and weak points of the unit; proposals and recommendations for improvement; and relevant quantitative indicators.

Criteria on Teaching Assessment. The instruction assessment report should include assessments of the program structure, teaching procedures, student and staff characteristics, and resources and outcomes.

Criteria on Research Assessment. Research is to be assessed in the following areas: the department's research objectives, human and material resources, research activity, productivity, quality indicators (see García, Mora, Pérez, and Rodríguez, 1995, where these indicators are defined), and research outcomes.

Criteria on Assessment of the Management of Units and Services. The assessment of management should focus on economic and administrative efficiency, decision-making procedures, student services structure, and facilities in general.

Consequences of the Evaluation Program on Quality Assurance Processes

By the end of 1997 some consequences from the first stage of the Evaluation Program could be identified. Generally speaking, in a relatively short time several important goals were reached. First, university leaders and staff now accept the evaluation process. The more these people know about and participate in the process, the more willing they are to accept assessment. Second, some of the improvement proposals are already being implemented, especially in the fields of teaching and management. Third, new offices to support these processes are being established rapidly in the universities. Finally, the publicity given to the whole process is promoting and stimulating a "quality culture" in universities.

These consequences are encouraging all institutions to develop more strategies for change and to provide clear support for improvement proposals. The main question now being raised by all participants is, What is the purpose, what are the tangible results, of these activities? If a satisfactory answer is not soon found, participants' interest and collaboration—which are crucial to this internal-external assessment methodology—will soon diminish. Because the required reports contain improvement proposals, they must soon result in some discernible consequences and rewards. Once needs are detected, institutions need to develop and implement improvement strategies, and it is difficult to go forward with improvements and additional assessment if the first stage—which is where these institutions are now—does not have any tangible consequences or rewards.

This situation has led some universities to move from quality assessment to quality assurance. Evaluation committees have now turned into permanent quality committees, and assessment processes are being included in the annual agendas of many institutions. This process is in its initial phase and there are already many differences in approach among the institutions. The involvement of institutional leaders in the movement for quality assurance is the main factor that determines the speed and intensity of these changes.

For example, the Technical University of Catalonia, one of the more active universities in the pilot project, has restructured its organization and its decision-making system around a strategic plan for quality. This plan has three stages (planning, execution, and evaluation) and affects both the institutional and unit levels. There are specific programs for human resources, budgetary policy, curriculum reform, environmental improvement, and so on. The University of Barcelona also has a quality plan containing five objectives: definition of its mission, evaluation of teaching and of research, a strategic plan for the improvement of management, and finally, improvement of information and its utilization by users.

The structure of these two plans or some of their components are found in other participating universities—from the oldest to the newest, and from the largest to the smallest. (Benchmarking is one of the most successful strategies in this initial stage.) The areas of common concern are always teaching (curriculum and syllabus design, new technologies, doctoral studies, and so on) and sometimes research, management, and services. Each university is adapting the Evaluation Program to its unique internal demands. For instance, the University of Salamanca has developed a plan for the evaluation of the whole university in two years. The University Carlos III (in Madrid) has a plan for quality based on TQM which stresses teaching and management. The University of Leon is attempting to carry out an evaluation and improvement program over three years. One of its most innovative objectives is the development of services for postgraduates. Mondragon University (Basque Country), which is focused on a program of technical studies and is one of the newest private universities in Spain, has obtained the ISO 9000 accreditation in standards of quality management. The University of the Basque Country is focusing on the training of quality teams (leaders, facilitators, and participants). Quality teams are the most commonly used methodology in the Evaluation Program. Examples of such efforts are found in almost every university. These programs represent a very dynamic situation involving many initiatives and a great degree of adaptation to the needs and possibilities of each institution, its needs, and its leadership.

Although there were local initiatives before the Evaluation Program was formalized, its implementation has had the consequence of moving institutions from the evaluation stage to the next level of quality improvement. Institutions that have supported the process with resources such as special units and technicians are moving definitively along the path to quality assurance. The coordination of these activities among different universities and the dissemination of information about the results and the consequences are very important next steps.

Finally, another consequence of the Evaluation Program has been the formal involvement of some more progressive regional governments in the process of stimulating quality assurance among institutions, eventually establishing regional agencies for promoting such quality efforts. An example is Catalonia's Agency for Quality in Universities, founded by the regional government and all the Catalan universities.

Conclusions

The move toward quality assurance in Spanish universities is recent but extremely positive and hopeful. In a few years it has been formally installed in the educational system and in the daily operations of a growing number of institutions. Nevertheless, the current process, for all its success, could be threatened by two dangers: bureaucratization and frustration.

First, a process such as this, with a central organization and dependent on a semigovernmental body such as the Council of Universities, could be considered by some people to be an additional formal, and perhaps unnecessary, requirement. The danger of bureaucratization of the process exists if it is not well explained and motivated. The capacity of the Council of Universities and other regional agencies to develop a dynamic structure to overcome these problems is crucial to the circumvention of this threat.

Second, the implementation of the recommendations and follow-up of the process are also essential. If people involved in the assessment and the university community in general do not feel that this is a worthwhile process with appropriate consequences and rewards, feelings of frustration with the process could be a danger for the future.

A mechanism, albeit not the only one, for keeping positive pressure on the quality assurance movement is to connect assessment results directly to funding. This is a very controversial issue that many policymakers and researchers do not recommend because it is regarded as a threat to the fairness of a process and system that should be solely "improvement focused" (Vroeijenstijn, 1995). Nevertheless, if universities are not compensated or rewarded in some fashion for attaining high standards of quality and performance, their commitment to quality assurance processes could be truncated. The biggest challenge, however, is to determine how to connect the results of these programs with funding. Several local initiatives could serve as examples. One such initiative, adopted in several regions, is the application of funding formulas that incorporate a variable related to quality in the allocation of public funds among universities (Mora and Villarreal, 1996). Another promising approach, adopted in other regions, is the use of contract-programs. This approach involves a contract between the regional government and each institution whereby universities are funded to achieve a set of specific goals. Such contracts are designed to reorganize the whole institution from the quality perspective. Whatever the method employed, a system of rewards and consequences are now needed to embed a quality assurance program firmly in Spanish universities for the new millennium.

References

Consejo de Universidades. *Programa de Evaluación Institucional de la Calidad de las Universidades* [Program for Institutional Evaluation of the Quality of the Universities]. Madrid: Consejo de Universidades, 1995.

Consejo de Universidades. *Informe Annual del Plan Nacional de Evaluacion de la Calidad de las Universidades* [Annual Report of the National Plan of Evaluation of the Quality of the Universities]. Madrid: Consejo de Universidades, 1998.

García, P., Mora, J. G., Pérez, J. J. and Rodríguez, S. "Experimenting with Institutional Evaluation in Spain." *Higher Education Management,* 1995, 7 (1) 111–118.

García-Garrido, J. L. "Spain." In B. R. Clark and G. Neave (eds.), *Encyclopedia of Higher Education,* Vol. 1. Oxford, England: Pergamon Press, 1992.

Hölttä, S. "Funding of Universities in Finland: Towards a Goal Oriented Government Steering." *European Journal of Education,* 1998, 33 (1), 55–63.

Layzell, D. "Linking Performance to Funding Outcomes for Public Institutions of Higher Education: The U.S. Experience." *European Journal of Education,* 1998, 33 (1), 103–111.

Mora, J. G. "The Demand for Higher Education in Spain." *European Journal of Education,* 1996, 31 (3), 341–354.

Mora, J. G. "Institutional Evaluation in Spain: An Ongoing Process." *Higher Education Management,* 1997a, 9 (1), 59–70.

Mora, J. G. "Market Trends in Spanish Higher Education." *Higher Education Policy,* 1997b, 10, (3/4), 187–198.

Mora, J. G., and Villarreal, E. "Funding for Quality: A New Deal in Spanish Higher Education." *Higher Education Policy,* 1996, 9 (2), 175–188.

Neave, G., and van Vught, F. *Prometheus Bound.* Oxford: Pergamon Press, 1991.

Vidal, J. "Transference and Interference Between Teaching and Research in the Spanish Universities." Paper presented at the Tenth Consortium of Higher Education Researchers Annual Meeting, Alicante, Spain, 1997.

Vroeijenstijn, A. I. *Improvement and Accountability: Navigating Between Scylla and Charybdis.* London: Jessica Kingsley Publisher, 1995.

Woodhouse, D. "Quality Assurance: International Trends, Preoccupations and Features." *Assessment and Evaluation in Higher Education,* 1996, 21 (4), 347–356.

JOSÉ-GINÉS MORA is professor of Economics at the University of Valencia, Spain, and a member of the National Committee of the Program for Institutional Evaluation of Quality in Universities.

JAVIER VIDAL is assistant professor of education and director of the Institutional Quality Program at the University of Leon, Spain.

Quality improvement and accountability are significant concerns for higher education in both the United Kingdom and the United States. This chapter outlines and compares the quality assurance processes in the two countries and identifies certain similarities and differences.

Quality Assurance in American and British Higher Education: A Comparison

Elizabeth C. Stanley, William J. Patrick

Quality assurance systems in the United Kingdom (England, Scotland, Wales, and Northern Ireland) and the United States reflect the differing cultures and traditions of the two countries and appear on the surface to be quite dissimilar. Upon closer inspection, however, a number of similarities emerge, despite the differences in size of the two systems.

Quality assurance systems may be classified as self-regulating (regulated by the institution or provider of the educational program), externally regulated (regulated by an external agency), or a combination of the two (mixed or collaborative regulation) (Kells, 1992; Jackson, 1997a). The United Kingdom's university system has moved rapidly away from self-regulation toward more mixed and externally imposed systems. The United States has also experienced an increasing emphasis on accountability and externally reported indicators, although voluntary accreditation remains an important form of self-regulation.

Higher education institutions in the United Kingdom are subject to overlapping systems of quality assurance for teaching and learning. New systems of external quality audit and quality assessment have supplemented a range of existing arrangements that include professional accreditation in certain subjects, regional accrediting consortia, interinstitutional subject-based networks, an external examiner system, and the internal quality control mechanisms within many institutions. With the formation in 1997 of the Quality Assurance Agency for Higher Education (QAAHE), steps were taken to rationalize quality assurance arrangements and to focus attention to a greater extent on standards of academic achievement. In addition to these systems of quality assurance for teaching and learning, the United Kingdom has also developed separate processes for research quality assessment.

Quality assurance processes in the United States take several forms, some of which are similar to those of the United Kingdom. Institutional accreditation and specialized accreditation provide evidence that institutions and programs are meeting certain minimum standards; they constitute the most prominent form of quality assurance in the United States. The role and processes of accreditation have been reexamined in recent years, and additional quality assurance systems have been developed or strengthened. These include performance indicator systems mandated by state agencies or governing boards, increased federal reporting requirements, expanded program review processes, and the publishing of program rankings.

The major processes for quality assurance in the United Kingdom and the United States are outlined in Tables 4.1 (U.K.) and 4.2 (U.S.) and are discussed in more detail in the following sections.

Quality Assurance Processes in the United Kingdom

The quality methods used by both sectors span several substantive and distinct arenas. Therefore, we begin by highlighting distinct arenas and presenting some specific principles and practices that apply to the approach being discussed.

Quality Audits. Quality audits in the United Kingdom were carried out by the Division of Quality Audit of the Higher Education Quality Council (HEQC) from 1993 until 1997. In 1997 the HEQC was subsumed within the new QAAHE.

The HEQC sought to support institutional self-regulation and to demonstrate to the system's various stakeholders that effective regulatory mechanisms were in place. It stressed that audits were not inspections and that they were not concerned with program validation, absolute academic standards, or institutional validation but instead were concerned with the procedures by which institutions assured themselves of the quality of their academic programs.

Today quality audits consider a wide range of factors: the institutional context; institutional systems and arrangements for quality assurance; the institutional design, approval, and review of programs of study; teaching, learning, and the student experience; student assessment and the classification of awards; student feedback and quality enhancement; faculty appointment, development, promotion, and reward; promotional materials for academic programs; and validation, franchising, and other forms of collaborative program provision (Higher Education Quality Council, 1993).

The auditing process consists of the provision of briefing material for an audit team, an audit visit, and an audit report. The briefing material includes a concise description of quality assurance arrangements at all levels in the institution, a brief analytical self-study of how these arrangements are seen to be working, and selected illustrative material. Audit reports are intended to be "temperate in tone" in order to encourage institutions to "continue to be

Table 4.1. Major Processes for Quality Assurance: United Kingdom

	Quality Audit	Teaching Quality Assessment	Research Assessment Exercise
Responsible agency	Higher Education Quality Council (HEQC) (institutions); moving to Quality Assurance Agency for Higher Education (QAAHE) (government and institutions)	Funding Council (government); moving to Quality Assurance Agency for Higher Education (QAAHE) (government and institutions)	Funding Councils (government)
Purpose	To support institutions' self-regulation by auditing the procedures by which they assure themselves of the quality of their academic provision	To ensure provision is of sufficient quality to justify public support, to improve quality, and to "inform" funding and reward excellence	Highly selective distribution of funds in support of high-quality research
Type of regulation (self, external, mixed)	Mixed	External	External
Scope (institution, department, program)	Institution	Subject area	Subject area
Activity assessed	Internal quality control mechanisms for teaching and learning	Teaching and learning	Research
Criteria (framework)	Nine broad aspects of institutions' quality control mechanisms	Six core aspects of subject provision (1995 onwards)	Research environment and plans
Standards	Mission-dependent	Mission-dependent	Adjudged national and international standards in each subject area
Evaluators	Predominantly peer review, with external assessors	Predominantly peer review, with external assessors drawn from the private sector and the professions	Predominantly peer review, with external assessors drawn from the private sector and the professions
Self-study	Yes (self-criticism encouraged)	Yes (self-criticism encouraged)	Yes (strengths highlighted; weaknesses downplayed)
Site visit	Yes	Yes	No
Indicators used	Predominantly textual material	Student entry profile, expenditure per student, progression and completion rates, qualifications attained, subsequent destinations	Peer-reviewed publications, research grant income, numbers of research assistants and students

(continued)

Table 4.1. (continued)

	Quality Audit	Teaching Quality Assessment	Research Assessment Exercise
Type of rating	Detailed written report, highlighting strengths and weaknesses	Each of six core aspects rated on a four-point scale (1995 onwards)	Seven categories, dependent on judgments concerning national and international standing
Dissemination	Funding Councils, institutions, potential consumers, press	Funding Councils, Web, institutions, potential consumers, press	Funding Councils, Web, institutions, potential consumers, press
Financial Impact	None	Funding withdrawn for persistent unsatisfactory provision; no reward so far (1997–98) for excellent provision	Profound: core funding focused on research excellence
Internal Impact	Significant; increasing: a more structured approach to quality control mechanisms	Significant; increasing: a more structured approach to the assurance of high-quality teaching and learning	Profound: organizational structure and management; faculty recruitment; teaching perhaps neglected
External Impact	Modest; increasing: dissemination of best practice and reports on findings published	Modest; increasing: dissemination of best practice and reports on findings published	Considerable: bandwagon effect as more research sponsors, faculty, and students are attracted to strong areas

Table 4.2. Major Processes for Quality Assurance: United States

	Regional Accreditation[a] / Specialized Accreditation	Performance Indicator Systems	Academic Program Review
Responsible agency	Six regional accrediting associations (voluntary associations of institutions); specialized and professional accrediting associations in more than fifty program areas	States, university systems, boards	Institutions, governing/coordinating boards
Purpose	To accredit institutions found to meet basic criteria, strengthen institutional and educational quality, advocate self-regulation through peer review, and provide information to the public	Accountability	Evaluation of the quality of an academic program or department
Type of regulation (self, external, mixed)	Mixed	External (although institutions may have voice in selection of indicators)	Self or mixed (board or state agency may establish requirements)
Scope (institution, department, program)	Institution (regional); unit, school, or program within an institution (specialized)	Primarily institutional, but may be used at departmental or program level	Academic program or department
Activity assessed	Overall quality of the institution or program; for specialized accreditation, focus on the professional preparation of the student	Institutional performance; efficiency and effectiveness	All program or department activities, including teaching, research, service/outreach
Criteria (framework)	General institutional requirements and criteria for accreditation; for specialized accreditation, professional or occupational requirements for the relevant area	State, system, or institutional goals in standard categories	Expectations for academic programs within the institution
Standards	Mission-dependent; vary by area for specialized accreditation	Vary	Vary by area
Evaluators	Peer review, with external assessors	Not applicable	Institutional faculty and administration; may be external peer review
Self-study	Yes	No	Yes, or similar report

(continued)

Table 4.2. (*continued*)

	Regional Accreditation[a] Specialized Accreditation	Performance Indicator Systems	Academic Program Review
Site visit	Yes	No	Yes, if peer review
Indicators used	Institutionally developed data on enrollment, student characteristics, faculty, finances, library, computing services, degree programs, athletics, student outcome measures	Vary; typically include measures of faculty quality and workload, graduation rates, student success, research support, publications, finance	Vary by area; typically enrollment, student characteristics, student outcomes, faculty productivity, budget, facilities
Type of rating	Accredited; candidate for accreditation, or on probation. Visiting team prepares report emphasizing strengths and challenges, and may offer advice and suggestions for institutional improvement	Tabulation of results; indication that goals are met or report of progress toward goals	Internal report with identification of strengths, weaknesses, and suggestions for improvement
Dissemination	Accreditation status published with basic institutional descriptors and any stipulations; team's report generally released only by institution	May be published as "report card"; may include comparisons with other institutions in system or state	Program or department and appropriate institutional administrators; may be reported to board or state
Financial impact	Significant; regional accreditation determines eligibility for federal funds	May affect state allocations of funds	Results may influence allocation of funds within institution
Internal impact	Significant, particularly when self-study process emphasizes institutional improvement	May result in policy and operational changes to address performance indicators	Significant for program improvement
External impact	Significant in student recruitment, eligibility for research funds; graduation from accredited program may be required for professional licensure	Major impact when required by governing/coordinating boards and used in their decision making	Major impact if required by governing/ coordinating boards and used in their decision making

Responsible agency	Institutions; may be required by governing/coordinating boards, states, and accrediting associations	National Research Council; sponsored by the Conference Board of Associated Research Councils	Publishers of various magazines and college guides
Purpose	To evaluate whether students have achieved the desired learning outcomes of their educational programs	To assess the effectiveness of doctoral programs in preparing graduates for careers in research and scholarship, to assist students in their choice of program, to inform administrators and policymakers, and to provide a database for further study	To provide information and ratings of educational programs and institutions
Type of regulation (self, external, mixed)	Self or mixed (board or state may establish requirements)	External	External
Scope (institution, department, program)	Degree program, department, institution	Research-doctorate programs in forty-one fields	Institutional or program
Activity assessed	Primarily teaching/learning; academic program and supporting services	Overall program characteristics with emphasis on research	Primarily undergraduate teaching and student life
Criteria (framework)	Achievement of desired learning outcomes of educational program	Scholarly quality of program faculty, effectiveness of program in educating research scholars/scientists; change in program quality in last five years; additional data on program characteristics	Adjudged quality, effectiveness, or efficiency of institution or program
Standards	Vary by area	Programs required to be of minimum size to be included in study	Vary
Evaluators	Faculty	Peer faculty raters	Sometimes reputational surveys of peers
Self-study	Not applicable	No	No
Site visit	Not applicable	No	No

(continued)

Table 4.2. (*continued*)

	Student Outcomes Assessment	Study of Research-Doctorate Programs	Publisher's Rankings
Indicators used	Vary by area; may include direct and indirect measures such as performance evaluations, examinations, surveys of alumni and employers	National survey of graduate faculty; data on number, rank and research support of faculty; publications, citations; student characteristics, doctorates produced, time to degree	Data collected from institutions and public sources; typically include enrollments, graduation rates, admissions data, costs, financial aid, academic programs, student activities
Type of rating	Report on measured student outcomes and the use of the results in improving educational processes	Rankings of programs within field by reputational ratings of scholarly quality of program faculty	Rankings or ratings of institutions/ programs, and/or the publication of information about them
Dissemination	Within program, department, institution and/or reports to governing/ coordinating board or state agency requiring the assessment; inclusion of results in program reviews and accreditation self-studies	Publication of rankings and extensive additional data in print and electronic forms; further research encouraged	Widespread by magazines, guidebooks, Web
Financial impact	Some state funding may be contingent on results	No direct impact	No direct impact
Internal impact	Most significant when used to improve teaching/learning processes, for curriculum revision and in program review and planning	Analysis of rankings and additional data may lead to program improvement	Minimal
External impact	Implementation of outcomes assessment procedures may be required by governing bodies and accreditation agencies	May influence choices by potential students and faculty	May influence student choice and public opinion

[a]Examples cited are for the North Central Association of Colleges and Schools, Commission on Institutions of Higher Education.

self-critical, and not to provoke defensiveness and inwardness" (Higher Education Quality Council, 1993, p. 9).

Quality Assessment. Quality assessment has been conducted separately by each of the funding councils in England (acting also for Northern Ireland), Scotland, and Wales. Assessment is of particular subjects rather than of whole institutions, as is the case in quality audits. This section focuses on the English experience (see Clark, 1997).

The purpose of quality assessment, as originally articulated by the Higher Education Funding Council for England (HEFCE), was "to ensure that all education for which the HEFCE provides funding is of satisfactory quality or better, and to ensure speedy rectification of unsatisfactory quality; to encourage improvements in the quality of education through the publication of assessment reports and an annual report; [and] to inform funding and reward excellence" (Higher Education Funding Council for England, 1993, p. 4). Quality is measured not against any absolute standards but rather against the aims and objectives set by institutions themselves. The process consists of a self-assessment, followed by peer review that includes a site visit (although these did not become universal until 1995) and a published report.

Self-assessments focus on the aims of the provider; on intended student learning experiences and achievements; on student, staff, and learning resources; and on an evaluation of the quality in each of six core aspects of provision: curriculum design, content and organization; teaching, learning, and assessment; student progression and achievement; student support and guidance; learning resources; and quality assurance and enhancement (Higher Education Funding Council for England, 1994). Self-assessments are expected to be self-critical and analytical rather than merely descriptive.

Each of the six core aspects of provision is graded on a four-point scale, with a grade of three or below identifying need for improvement. Funding can be withdrawn if quality remains unsatisfactory after twelve months.

Standards-Based Quality Assurance. The United Kingdom's systems of external scrutiny of teaching and learning are currently changing significantly in order to combine and simplify the external quality assessment and quality audit procedures, and to address concern over the educational standards attained by graduates. The National Committee of Inquiry into Higher Education (NCIHE), charged with making wide-ranging recommendations about the future of higher education in the United Kingdom, echoed the frustrations that developed after the Further and Higher Education Act of 1992 increased the size and diversity of the system. Employers were especially concerned about the variation and lack of clarity in the standards of achievement in the awards made by different institutions. The committee saw the way forward "lying in the development of common standards, specified and verified through a strengthened external examiner system, supported by a lighter approach to quality assessment" (National Committee of Inquiry into Higher Education, 1997, p. 157). This would, it was believed, reduce the load borne by institutions. There was also a warning: "In the absence of the infrastructure and arrangements of the kind we propose, pressures for increased and direct intervention from outside [the] higher education system will intensify" (National Committee of Inquiry into Higher Education, 1997, p. 164). The NCIHE advocated the establishment of a national framework of qualifications—recognizing, however, that the present distinctiveness of the Scottish system would prevent this from happening in the short term. (See Chapter Five in this volume, by Chris Carter and Alan Davidson.) The committee recommended that the framework should have "a standardized nomenclature for awards; agreed and common credit points at relevant levels; [and] the inclusion of additional and recognized 'stopping-off' points" (National Committee of Inquiry into Higher Education, 1997, p. 151).

The change of emphasis may be characterized as a change from a concern primarily with the quality of the educational process and students' learning experiences to a concern mainly with the quality of the outcomes of the educational process (Jackson, 1998). It is likely that in addition to establishing a qualifications framework, this shift will entail the use of threshold standards developed within the higher education sector that specify the intellectual characteristics of individuals who complete particular types of programs, and individual program specifications drawn up by their providers that define content.

Quality Assessment of Research.   Research quality in higher education institutions in the United Kingdom has been evaluated through four national research assessment exercises (RAEs), in 1986, 1989, 1992, and 1996. Central government funding is distributed selectively on the basis of quality, and the main purpose of the RAEs is to produce the quality ratings on which the funding councils make resource allocation decisions. In each exercise, institutions have submitted standard statistical and narrative material to central, specialist panels for peer review. The information considered by the panels has been purely documentary. Site visits and reputational ratings have not been used (Patrick and Stanley, 1996, 1998).

In the 1996 research assessment exercise, each institution could make a submission in any of sixty-nine units of assessment, defined to cover a full range of academic disciplines, including clinical medicine and dentistry. Since the inception of the assessment exercises, panels have come to place increased emphasis on the research publications presented by faculty as their best work during the relevant assessment period. The adjudged quality of these publications, along with other information provided by institutions, has formed the basis of the quality ratings that in 1996 were awarded on a seven-point, criterion-referenced scale based on the attainment of national and international levels of excellence.

Institutions have suggested that the benefits of formal research assessment include "improvements in the research quality and in the strategic management of research; a more dynamic research environment; and greater accountability." Certain disadvantages have also been identified: "the financial cost and human effort of conducting frequent RAEs; pressure on researchers to produce new published outcomes in time for each successive exercise; effects upon academic activities not covered by RAE, including both teaching and scholarship; [and] the development of RAE-driven recruitment practices as higher education institutions seek to better their RAE ratings" (Higher Education Funding Councils, 1997, p. 2).

Other Forms of Quality Assurance in the United Kingdom. The role of external examiners in the United Kingdom has been to ensure that degrees awarded in similar subjects by different institutions are comparable in standard, and that students are treated fairly by institutions' internal systems of assessment and classification. The independence and objectivity of external examiners are much valued, but the increased size and diversity of the higher education sector has put the external examiner system under considerable strain, and additional mechanisms are being developed to strengthen and supplement their efforts. (For another perspective on the external examiner system, see Chapter Five in this volume, by Carter and Davidson.) Professional accreditation processes in the United Kingdom are similar to those in the United States.

Although there is a growing literature available to the public on higher education, its effect on student choice appears to be limited at present.

Quality Assurance Processes in the United States

As with Great Britain, U.S. quality assurance processes span several substantive and distinct arenas, and the boundaries of application are not always well defined. For each presentation, we discuss the items as distinct entities; in reality, however, they fall on continua.

Regional Accreditation. Accreditation is the major process for quality assurance in higher education in the United States, and the ability to exercise self-regulation through accreditation is viewed as an important part of the heritage of U.S. higher education (Ikenberry, 1997). Accreditation involves voluntary peer review and is carried out by nongovernmental regional and specialized accrediting agencies. Six regional accrediting associations of colleges and schools and several national associations for particular types of schools (such as religious schools) provide accreditation at the institutional level. The federal government uses regional accreditation to determine the eligibility of an institution for federal funding.

Regional accreditation is intended to certify that institutions meet certain basic resource and performance criteria, to strengthen educational quality, to encourage self-examination, to support self-regulation, and to assure the public that an institution meets certain minimum standards of quality. Institutional accreditation evaluates institutions with respect to their missions and attempts to recognize and support institutional diversity and autonomy. The process is typically based on a ten-year cycle, with an extensive institutional self-study followed by a site visit by a team of peer reviewers. The team's report addresses both the accountability and the improvement functions of accreditation by making a recommendation regarding the institution's accreditation status and emphasizing both the strengths of the institution and its challenges. The report may also include advice and suggestions to the institution for improvement.

Accreditation processes and requirements vary slightly among the six regional accrediting bodies. The Commission on Institutions of Higher Education of the North Central Association of Colleges and Schools specifies twenty-four general institutional requirements concerned with mission, authorization, governance, faculty, educational programs, finances, and public information. An institution must also demonstrate that it satisfies five criteria for accreditation relating to the appropriateness of its purposes and mission, the effective use of resources, the accomplishment of its purposes, the ability to continue to accomplish its purposes, and institutional integrity (North Central Association Commission on Institutions of Higher Education, 1997).

Several national accrediting organizations conduct similar processes for specific types of institutions, such as theological schools, bible colleges, and health education schools. A larger number of organizations provide specialized and professional accreditation, discussed in the next section.

The Council on Higher Education Accreditation was established in 1996 as a nonprofit organization of colleges and universities. It is supported by the institutions and by the regional, national, and specialized accrediting agencies. It recognizes accrediting bodies, serves as an advocate for voluntary self-regulation through accreditation, conducts research and disseminates information about accreditation, and fosters communication among the accrediting bodies and the higher education community.

Specialized Accreditation. Specialized and professional accrediting associations employ similar processes in the accreditation of particular units, schools, or programs within institutions. More than fifty such associations evaluate programs in such professions as law, medicine, and engineering, and in specific disciplines such as computer science, journalism, and psychology. Graduation from an accredited program may be required for national or state licensure or advancement in a professional area. Also, the lack of such accreditation may have a substantial impact on an institution's ability to secure external research funding.

Performance Indicator Systems. Increasing demands for accountability by the public, legislatures, and governing and coordinating boards have led to the development of externally driven quantitative performance indicator systems at the level of state or university systems. In 1996–97, thirty-seven states reported the use of performance measures in higher education, and seven additional states indicated that they were planning to implement performance measure systems in the near future (Christal, 1998). Performance measures were used in the distribution of funds to institutions by twenty-three of the states reporting in 1996–97, and eight states indicated that some portion of institutions' state allocations were linked directly to performance measures. Such indicators help to demonstrate an institution's progress toward or achievement of institutional, system, or state goals, but the relationship of the indicators to the learning environment and their usefulness in program improvement are questionable (Nedwek and Neal, 1994). The characteristics of effective performance indicator systems have been summarized by Gaither (1997).

Academic Program Review. The practice of academic program review has been widely accepted within U.S. institutions and represents an important form of internal quality assurance. It is comparable to internal quality assurance procedures in the United Kingdom (such as those described by Carter and Davidson in Chapter Five of this volume). Barak and Sweeney (1995) reported that 83 percent of the institutions responding to a 1993–94 survey used a systematic program review process, and that a majority used the results for program improvement. More than three-quarters of the respondents reported the use of program review in institutional planning and budgeting, and most indicated the successful integration of program review, planning, and budgeting. Critics have suggested, however, that current program review processes should be strengthened by the more rigorous application of specific measures in order to provide more effective internal quality assurance (Dill, Massey, Williams, and Cook, 1996).

Academic program review processes established by institutions usually operate on a five-year cycle, with periodic reviews conducted at the program or department level. The results of program reviews may be reported to a governing board or state system, thus providing an additional measure of accountability. Similar procedures have been adopted for administrative program review in some institutions and systems.

Student Outcomes Assessment. Student outcomes assessment is increasingly important in providing a measure of quality and is an important component of some broad quality assurance activities. Public interest in outcomes measurement is also increasing, particularly in such measures as graduation rates and job placement data. Although accrediting agencies and coordinating and governing boards may require the assessment of student outcomes, it is generally agreed that a successful assessment program must be developed and implemented by faculty, and that the results must be used for the improvement of academic programs as well as for external accountability.

An effective assessment program is based on the institutional mission and on the identification by faculty of the expected outcomes of an academic program. Student learning may be evaluated by both direct measures (such as portfolio assessments, evaluation of capstone courses or senior theses, examinations, and evaluation of performance) and indirect measures (such as graduation rates, surveys of alumni and employers, and job placement data). Multiple measures are recommended, and effective feedback should be provided to both students and faculty.

Rankings of Research-Doctorate Programs. Rankings of institutions or programs can provide indicators of perceived quality. Studies of research-doctorate programs published in 1966, 1970, 1982, and 1995 have rated doctoral programs on the basis of reputational measures and selected quantitative factors. The 1995 report ranked programs by field on the basis of "scholarly quality of program faculty" (Goldberger, Maher, and Flattau, 1995, p. 22). It included 3,634 programs in forty-one fields at 274 U.S. universities. The study was conducted by a committee appointed by the National Research Council under the aegis of the Conference Board of Associated Research Councils. It sought to evaluate the effectiveness of doctoral programs in preparing graduates for careers in research and scholarship, to provide students with assistance in the selection of an appropriate program, and to provide information to administrators and policymakers.

A national survey of graduate faculty was conducted to obtain reputational ratings of each program's "scholarly quality of program faculty," the "effectiveness of the program in educating research scholars," and the "change in program quality in the last five years" (Goldberger, Maher, and Flattau, 1995, p. 22). Additional data were compiled on program characteristics, including the number of faculty, their awards and honors, research support, publications and citations, student characteristics, and information about doctoral recipients. Some of the data were provided by the institutions, but most were available through national databases. Institutional self-studies and site visits were not undertaken.

Publishers' Rankings. Undergraduate programs and institutions have been ranked or rated in a number of U.S. magazines and college guides, including *U.S. News & World Report, Money* magazine, and the *Fiske Guide to Colleges.* Other publishers provide information about and ratings of institutions and their programs without explicit rankings. Graduate and professional programs are becoming the subject of similar rankings and guides. The rankings are based primarily on the analysis of institutionally supplied data and, in some cases, reputational data collected through surveys of students or institutional administrators. The various publications differ greatly in their criteria for rankings and the data collected, although a group of publishers and professional associations has recently developed a common data set to standardize the definitions of some data elements (College Board, 1998). Hunter (1995) has suggested that "U.S. News' annual rankings have set the public agenda for determining quality in higher education" (p. 10), although the validity of the published conclusions is often questioned within the educational community. In Chapter One of this volume, E. Grady Bogue cites student poll evidence that student choice of a university in the United States is only minimally affected by such information.

Other Forms of Quality Assurance in the United States. Internal quality assurance approaches can include the assessment of institutional effectiveness and more generic management techniques such as TQM and Continuous Quality Improvement. Bogue and Saunders (1992) add licensure and alumni follow-up studies as additional instruments of quality assurance.

Common Issues and Future Directions

The distinctiveness and complexity of the quality assurance mechanisms outlined in this chapter are indicative of the evolution of individual processes to serve widely differing circumstances and publics in the United Kingdom and the United States. Various common concerns and the sharing of mechanisms used, however, are leading to greater similarity between the two systems.

Costs. There are deep concerns over the cost of higher education in both countries. In the United Kingdom, the NCIHE owes its origins mainly to the financial crisis in the higher education sector. The need to identify new sources of revenue resulted in the committee's recommendation that for the first time U.K. students should contribute to the payment of their own tuition. In the United States, concerns with the rising costs of higher education have led to increasing attention to productivity and attempts to establish additional external regulating bodies, such as the now-rejected State Postsecondary Review Entities.

Mission Difference. Differences in such areas as institutional mission and diversity have increased dramatically in both countries: in the United Kingdom, differences have occurred as the numbers of both universities and students have increased, and in the United States changes have resulted from the increasing use of technology, distance learning, and new providers. Because of this greater complexity, members of the public now look for more comparative information, and they support and use the proliferation of rankings and guidebook information available in the public domain. The preparation of "report cards" of performance indicators in the United States and the NCIHE's call for a system of generally recognized academic standards in the United Kingdom are further evidence of the response to and demand for information to assist consumers in choosing among diverse options. To respond to increased diversity, quality assurance systems will need to develop new and different approaches to the judgment of quality, both for traditional higher education programs and for those based on alternative structures and technologies (Ikenberry, 1997). (See Chapter Six of this volume, by John E. Neal, for specific efforts being developed by entrepreneurial institutions.)

Accountability and Regulation. In both countries, the regulatory framework has become more elaborate and formalized, and there has been a tendency for new external and mixed forms of quality assurance to be superimposed on existing internal arrangements, in some cases by legislation. Internal processes for self-regulation, such as the external examiner system in the United Kingdom and student outcomes assessment in the United States, are also being strengthened in response to greater external pressures. The demand for greater accountability in the use of funds is one of the main driving forces behind the changes taking place in higher education on both sides of the Atlantic.

Improvement and Enhancement. Program improvement and enhancement are encouraged in both countries. The English system of teaching quality assessment and the United Kingdom's system of quality audit seek to improve quality through the publication of findings and the dissemination of best practices. The preparation of internal self-assessments as part of these approaches has the most potential to provide an immediate and effective mechanism for achieving improvement in teaching and learning. Similarly, respondents to a survey concerning regional accreditation processes in the United

States indicated that the institutional self-study is the most useful part of the accreditation process (North Central Association Commission on Institutions of Higher Education, 1998). Regional accrediting agencies such as the North Central Association and the Southern Association of Colleges and Schools are exploring alternative procedures, including quality audits similar to those of the United Kingdom, to maximize the value of the process for the institutions.

Student outcomes assessment in the United States is focused mainly on improvement, although many assessment programs were initiated in response to external accountability requirements. Proposals for standards-based quality assurance in the United Kingdom involve similar assessments of expected student learning outcomes (Quality Assurance Agency for Higher Education, 1998).

Integration. Attempts are being made on both sides of the Atlantic to achieve greater integration of quality assurance mechanisms. Bogue and Saunders (1992) recommend an integrated quality assurance model that will serve the needs of both accountability and improvement; Middlehurst (1997) discusses a framework that considers accountability, development, and market principles. In the United Kingdom, the establishment of the QAAHE to address quality, audit and standards issues is tangible evidence of the move toward integration. Examples in the United States include the establishment of the Council on Higher Education Accreditation, collaboration among regional accrediting agencies in the evaluation of distance learning programs, proposals for increased collaboration between regional and specialized accrediting agencies, and the increased use of student outcomes assessment within accreditation, program review, and performance indicator systems. A higher level of integration may be more attainable in the United Kingdom, where higher education remains more a national system than in the United States with its variation among states, its strong private sector, and a traditional emphasis on the uniqueness of institutional missions. In Chapter Six of this volume, Neal discusses the incipient efforts of entrepreneurial institutions to develop and integrate quality assurance mechanisms.

Tensions. Regulation tends to be an external concern, whereas improvement has generally been acknowledged to be primarily the internal responsibility of individual institutions. Externally imposed systems have usually not been well accepted by internal stakeholders and have been more effective for regulation than for quality improvement (Gaither, 1997). There have been various calls to reduce tensions between the requirements of the different stakeholders in higher education and between internal and external quality assurance processes. In the United Kingdom, the NCIHE (1997) has advocated a fundamental redrawing of the customer-supplier relationship in higher education to create a new compact among students, institutions, the economy, employers, and the state in which all parties are expected to benefit. In the United States, Graham, Lyman, and Trow (1995) have argued that improvement depends on self-criticism and effective internal reviews with greater attention to teaching and learning. External reviews (by accrediting bodies) should then take the form of academic audits of the institution's internal quality control processes. Jackson (1997b) similarly proposes a shift in the United Kingdom from external accountability reviews to an emphasis on self-criticism and internal review with appropriate external safeguards.

Conclusion

Despite their differences in culture and tradition, the United Kingdom and the United States have established quality assurance processes with increasingly common features. Useful parallels and contrasts may be drawn between the two. With continuing dialogue, each will be able to learn from the other, and their various publics will be the greatest beneficiaries of the continuing development of effective quality assurance processes.

References

Barak, R. J., and Sweeney, J. D. "Academic Program Review in Planning, Budgeting, and Assessment." In R. J. Barak and L. A. Mets (eds.), *Using Academic Program Review.* New Directions for Institutional Research, no. 86. San Francisco: Jossey-Bass, 1995.

Bogue, E. G., and Saunders, R. L. *The Evidence for Quality.* San Francisco: Jossey-Bass, 1992.

Christal, M. E. "State Survey on Performance Measures: 1996–97." *Network News, A Quarterly Bulletin of the SHEEO/NCES Communication Network,* 1998, *17* (1), 1–3.

Clark, P. M. "Reflections on Quality Assessment in England: 1993–1996." *Quality Assurance in Education,* 1997, *5* (4), 218–224.

College Board. "Common Data Set." [http://www.collegeboard.org/gp/html/common-dataset.html]. Accessed Apr. 12, 1998.

Dill, D. D., Massey, W. F., Williams, P. R., and Cook, C. M. "Accreditation and Academic Quality Assurance: Can We Get There From Here?" *Change,* 1996, *28* (5), 17–24.

Gaither, G. H. "Performance Indicator Systems as Instruments for Accountability and Assessment." *Assessment Update,* 1997, *9* (1), 1–2, 14–15.

Goldberger, M. L., Maher, B. A., and Flattau, P. E. (eds.). *Research-Doctorate Programs in the United States: Continuity and Change.* Washington, D.C.: National Academy Press, 1995.

Graham, P. A., Lyman, R. W., and Trow, M. *Accountability of Colleges and Universities.* New York: Columbia University, 1995.

Higher Education Funding Council for England. *Assessment of the Quality of Education.* Circular 3/93. Bristol: Higher Education Funding Council for England, 1993.

Higher Education Funding Council for England. *The Quality Assessment Method from April 1995.* Circular 39/94. Bristol: Higher Education Funding Council for England, 1994.

Higher Education Funding Council. *Research Assessment: Consultation.* Circular RAE 2/97. Bristol: Higher Education Funding Council, 1997.

Higher Education Quality Council, Division of Quality Audit. *Notes for the Guidance of Auditors.* Birmingham, England: Higher Education Quality Council, 1993.

Hunter, B. "College Guidebooks: Background and Development." In R. D. Walleri and M. K. Moss (eds.), *Evaluating and Responding to College Guidebooks and Rankings.* New Directions for Institutional Research, no. 88. San Francisco: Jossey-Bass, 1995.

Ikenberry, S. O. "Defining a New Agenda: Higher Education and the Future of America." *NCA Quarterly,* 1997, *71* (4), 445–450.

Jackson, N. "Academic Regulation in UK Higher Education. Part I: The Concept of Collaborative Regulation." *Quality Assurance in Education,* 1997a, *5* (3), 120–135.

Jackson, N. "Academic Regulation in UK Higher Education. Part II: Typologies and Frameworks for Discourse and Strategic Change." *Quality Assurance in Education,* 1997b, *5* (3), 165–179.

Jackson, N. "Conceptual Basis for Standards-Based Quality Assurance." Background paper for Quality Assurance and Enhancement Network Conference, Coventry, England, Feb. 11–12, 1998.

Kells, H. R. *Self-Regulation in Higher Education: A Multi-National Perspective on Collaborative Systems of Quality Assurance and Control.* London: Jessica Kingsley Publishers, 1992.

Middlehurst, R. "Quality Enhancement for Accountability and Transformation: A Framework for the Future." *Tertiary Education and Management,* 1997, 3 (1), 15–24.

National Committee of Inquiry into Higher Education. *Higher Education in the Learning Society, Main Report.* London: Her Majesty's Stationery Office, 1997.

Nedwek, B. P., and Neal, J. E. "Performance Indicators and Rational Management Tools: A Comparative Assessment of Projects in North America and Europe." *Research in Higher Education,* 1994, 35 (1), 75–103.

North Central Association Commission on Institutions of Higher Education. *Handbook of Accreditation.* (2nd ed.) Chicago: North Central Association Commission on Institutions of Higher Education, 1997.

North Central Association Commission on Institutions of Higher Education. *Effective Collaboration for the Twenty-First Century: The Commission and Its Stakeholders.* Chicago: North Central Association Commission on Institutions of Higher Education, 1998.

Patrick, W. J., and Stanley, E. C. "Assessment of Research Quality." *Research in Higher Education,* 1996, 37 (1), 23–42.

Patrick, W. J., and Stanley, E. C. "Teaching and Research Quality Indicators and the Shaping of Higher Education." *Research in Higher Education,* 1998, 39 (1), 19–41.

Quality Assurance Agency for Higher Education. *Higher Quality: Consultation Issue.* London: Quality Assurance Agency for Higher Education, 1998.

ELIZABETH C. STANLEY *is director of institutional research at Iowa State University, Ames, Iowa.*

WILLIAM J. PATRICK *is planning officer of the University of Glasgow, Scotland.*

Although higher education in Scotland is part of the U.K. system, it has operated separately, with a distinctive focus on the assessment of quality in each academic subject.

Quality Assurance in Scottish Higher Education

Chris Carter, Alan Davidson

For the purposes of this chapter, the term *quality assurance* is taken to embrace the various activities by which the Scottish public higher education system as a whole assures itself that the quality of education provided in each institution meets the stated objectives. Some of these activities are for the most part conducted internally by the institutions themselves; others are primarily conducted externally by other bodies. The focus in this chapter is on quality assurance in relation to teaching and learning, not on quality assurance for research. The latter is undertaken every four years through a research assessment exercise that is discussed elsewhere in this volume (see Chapter Four by Elizabeth Stanley and William Patrick).

Background

Some background information will provide the context for our analysis of quality assurance in Scottish higher education. First, the Scottish system is small, with only twenty-one higher education institutions and a total full-time equivalent student population in 1997–98 of approximately 140,000. Thirteen of the twenty-one institutions are universities. The remaining eight are small institutions that specialize in particular vocational subject areas such as teacher training, art and design, the performing arts, or health and food studies. A number of merger proposals currently under consideration will likely, if approved, bring some of these smaller institutions into the university fold and reduce the overall number of institutions to eighteen by 1998–99.

Second, all Scottish higher education institutions are publicly funded, although the level of dependency on public funds (including fees for tuition, which for most students are also publicly funded) varies from about 50 percent to 95 percent of the total budget. The institutions that are the least dependent on public funds are those with the highest incomes from private or charity-sponsored research. The teaching and learning elements in all institutions are heavily dependent on public funding.

Third, prior to the 1992 Further and Higher Education Act, the Scottish higher education system was less easily identifiable as a separate system because it was more fully integrated into the United Kingdom's higher education system, although it remains part of that system. Prior to 1992 the Scottish higher education system was clearly divided into two parts: the university sector and the nonuniversity or "central institution" sector. At that time there were only eight universities in Scotland and seventeen nonuniversity institutions. Five of these seventeen institutions have since become universities, and four have ceased to exist as separate institutions after merging with others.

Following the implementation of the 1992 Higher Education Act, three main forms of quality assurance activity were utilized for the teaching and learning activities in Scottish higher education institutions. The first activity was *internal quality assurance,* undertaken by the individual institutions; the second was the *external quality audit,* conducted by the Higher Education Quality Council (HEQC) to ensure that institutions had implemented effective internal quality control procedures; and the third was the *subject-by-subject teaching quality assessments* undertaken by the Scottish Higher Education Funding Council (SHEFC) to ensure that the internal procedures were producing the desired results.

Internal Quality Assurance Procedures and Quality Audit

All Scottish higher education institutions now have internal quality assurance procedures in place and all have participated in at least one round of quality audits. The first round of audits was completed in 1996–97 and the second round began in 1997–98. No alarm bells have been rung as far as Scottish institutions are concerned, and it can be assumed that the HEQC, now absorbed into a new agency (the Quality Assurance Agency for Higher Education, or QAAHE), has been generally content with the internal quality assurance procedures that have been implemented in each higher education institution in Scotland.

The procedures used in our own institution, the University of Dundee, are not greatly different from those of other institutions and can be used as an illustrative example. The overall aim of the quality assurance procedures is to help the university fulfill its mission, which includes, among other things, the intention "to provide education of the highest quality" (University of Dundee,

1998). The procedures are incorporated in the university's academic standards scheme. Its main elements are the following:

The adoption of a formal quality assurance policy as a statement of the university's commitment to implementing such procedures as part of its pursuit of excellence

The establishment of appropriate committee structures to oversee the implementation of the policy

A commitment to the participation of students in the procedures, especially through the annual completion of student satisfaction questionnaires for each course taught, but also through their involvement in departmental student-staff consultative committees

The creation of formal procedures for the periodic and systematic review of programs and courses

The use of formal procedures for the approval of new or extensively revised programs and courses

The requirement that all departments participate in the peer support of teaching

The use of a clear code for the supervision of postgraduate provision

The establishment of procedures for monitoring the reports of the many professional accreditation bodies with which the university has relations, and for ensuring that, where appropriate, the recommendations of such bodies are implemented

The application of these policies to distance learning and other off-campus programs that lead to the award of qualifications by the university

There is little doubt that the introduction and implementation of such procedures in all Scottish higher education institutions has done much to generate an explicit concern with the quality of teaching and learning, and has resulted in a greater recognition that all institutions are accountable for the quality of the educational experiences they offer. The effectiveness with which such institutional procedures are implemented varies considerably, however, not only among institutions but also among the different parts of the same institutions. To some extent this may reflect the different ways in which various institutions, or parts of institutions, have modified their behavior simply to respond to the external requirements placed on them. Nevertheless, in general faculty have developed a willingness to be reflective about what they do and about the context within which they do it.

The value of such changes must, however, be measured against the considerable costs of implementing the procedures, especially in terms of staff time. Most institutions have found it necessary to establish special units, sometimes involving several staff members, to coordinate and oversee the quality assurance activities. In addition, many academic and senior management staff, together with the necessary administrative support, commit a great deal of their time to undertaking and documenting the various activities and participating in the accompanying committee work. Thus the drain on scarce funds and time has been the major downside to the quality assurance process in Scottish higher education.

At two points in the first cycle of quality audits the HEQC published reports under the title *Learning from Audit* (HEQC, 1994, 1996). Although these reports apply to the United Kingdom as a whole, their main findings are generally applicable to the higher education sector in Scotland. The reports note that most institutions are now effectively implementing audit procedures, but they express a number of concerns that remain to be addressed, most notably the following:

The link between design and approval of programs and resource allocation

The evaluation of teaching and learning, including the use of student and other sources of feedback

Staff recruitment, promotion, and training, including in particular clear links between evaluation of teaching and staff appraisal and promotion

Student assessment, including the use of external examiners

The challenges posed by the introduction of modularity (unit-based programs)

The pressures being placed on limited resources for learning and support activities

The risks of greater variations in both accountability and enhancement across institutions, resulting from a devolution of centralized quality control to individual schools and faculties

The need for institutions to control the accuracy of promotional material

As a result of these findings, along with the emergence of pressures from the government to tackle the issue of standards in higher education, the audit visits that were begun during the past year have changed considerably from those performed in the previous round. Attention is now focused on two key questions: How do institutions set the standards for the courses and programs they offer? and How do institutions assure themselves that these standards are being met? At the time of the writing of this chapter it is premature to comment on how well this new approach has been implemented or to indicate the main findings.

External Teaching Quality Assessment

The effectiveness with which internal quality assurance has been implemented by individual institutions has been influenced significantly since 1992–93, when the SHEFC introduced subject-by-subject teaching quality assessments (TQAs). It became apparent soon after their implementation that a factor receiving much attention in the TQA visits was whether an institution could indicate how well the quality of teaching and learning was being maintained or enhanced as a result of its own quality assurance procedures. Above all, hard evidence was being sought by assessors to substantiate any claims of excellence that were being made. As time progressed, institutions were expected to demonstrate in each subject area that a general culture of commitment to the procedures existed among staff and students.

The SHEFC's intention in introducing TQAs was to assess all or most "cognate areas" (that is, single subjects or groups of closely related subjects) over a five-year cycle. The cycle was extended, however, by one year and was completed during the 1997–98 academic year. The key principles of the TQAs during the first cycle were as follows (Scottish Higher Education Funding Council, 1993a, 1993b):

1. The cognate areas to be assessed would be advised approximately one year in advance.
2. Approximately six months in advance of the proposed visit, institutions would be invited to submit a self-assessment document for each cognate area.
3. The self-assessment would be structured to follow a detailed set of guidelines focusing in particular on a "quality framework" that cited eleven dimensions of quality. These dimensions were as follows:
    a. Aims and curricula
    b. Curriculum design and review
    c. The teaching and learning environment
    d. Staff resources
    e. Learning resources
    f. Course organization
    g. Teaching and learning practice
    h. Student support
    i. Assessment and monitoring
    j. Students' work
    k. Outputs, outcomes and quality control
    l. Student placement (added for some cognate areas in which professional practice plays a significant role)
4. Institutions could submit such supporting documentation as they deemed necessary.
5. A "previsit" would take place about one month before the actual site visit to establish the program, identify any particular items that might be the focus of attention, and indicate whether any further supporting documentation was required.
6. The three-to-four-day visit would involve a team of about five assessors, drawn mostly from peer academics nominated by all the Scottish institutions being assessed in the cognate area. The visiting assessors usually would include one from the United Kingdom outside of Scotland and one industrial-professional assessor. All assessors would have received training from the SHEFC.
7. The site visit would involve meetings with groups of staff and students, including senior management staff and those responsible for operating support services. Approximately half of the visiting assessors' time in any site visit would be spent directly observing teaching and learning.

8. At the end of each visit, the assessor team would meet privately to discuss their findings and come to a decision about the overall quality of provision using a four-point grading scale: excellent, highly satisfactory, satisfactory, and unsatisfactory.

9. About two months later a draft report would be sent to the institution that would not yet reveal the actual gradings awarded by the assessors for the various dimensions of the quality framework. This transmittal would be followed closely by a postvisit meeting at which the institution could draw attention to any matters of factual inaccuracy in the report and could subsequently submit any points in writing if it wished.

10. In another two months the report would be published with all the reports on other institutions offering education in the same cognate area. These reports would be widely circulated to the media and to all secondary schools and colleges in Scotland.

11. Any institution receiving a grade of "excellent" would be rewarded with a recurrent increased funding allocation, equivalent to 5 percent of the existing government funding committed to the institution for students in that cognate area. Any institution receiving an "unsatisfactory" grade would be required to review its program and submit a new self-assessment within a year. A site revisit would then take place. If that visit were successful, the cognate area would be regraded "satisfactory" (but not higher); if the visit were unsuccessful, the "unsatisfactory" grade would be reconfirmed and funding could thereafter be withdrawn.

12. The SHEFC would publish an annual report summarizing all the main findings and grades received (on the four-point grade scale) in the assessments carried out in the various cognate areas during the previous year.

This approach, together with the details of the quality framework, was devised in consultation with the institutions before implementation. Although there have been some misgivings by the institutions, they have recognized the statutory requirement that quality assessments must be conducted, and that some form of assessment is unavoidable. Given this attitude and, as noted earlier, that TQAs played an important part in ensuring that institutions implement their own quality assurance procedures effectively, it might at first glance be assumed that there would be a generally high level of satisfaction with quality assessment in Scotland among the participating institutions. This is not the case, however, and a number of concerns have arisen.

First, from the outset the SHEFC's stated general aims of quality assessment have been as follows:

To inform the SHEFC about the quality of teaching and learning in the full range of subjects offered by institutions of higher education for which it provides funding

To produce reports from the assessment visits that highlight the strengths and weaknesses of teaching and learning

To inform potential students, employers, and the general public about the quality of teaching and learning in all subject areas

To help disseminate good practices observed by assessors among all institutions and thereby encourage continuous quality improvement

These aims make it evident that concern has been focused on identifying where the best and worst provisions in any subject area are offered, identifying particular strengths and weaknesses in programs, and informing the so-called stakeholders. Quality enhancement, which the institutions have regarded as the most important aim, has been relegated to last place. As a result, and in view of the additional funding that has been offered to departments that secure an "excellent" rating, quality assessments have become highly competitive, strongly reinforcing the competitiveness that had already been engendered through the overall funding mechanisms for teaching and the four-year research assessment exercise.

Second, teams of assessors have been drawn largely (but not entirely) from institutions within Scotland. This has heightened the competitiveness issue because such individuals have been assessing operations and programs in institutions with which their own institutions are in competition for students. Furthermore, some subject areas are taught in only a few institutions, which has the potential to increase the significance of this issue; it is, after all, only human nature to be somewhat reluctant to concede competitive advantage by awarding higher gradings to direct competitors. Although the SHEFC recognized that assessors would have to be drawn from further afield in, for example, dentistry and veterinary medicine (which are taught in only two institutions), the council otherwise chose to play down the competitiveness issue by emphasizing the professional integrity of its Scottish assessors.

Third, evidence—anecdotal as well as hard results of studies—suggests that different teams of assessors have taken very different approaches, both in their desire to expose weaknesses and in their approach to awarding grades (Entwistle, 1995). Coupled with the concerns of competitiveness just discussed, these differences have produced some rather inconsistent results. For example, in geography there were four "excellent" grades out of six, but in civil engineering there were none out of ten; in chemistry there were six "excellents" out of twelve, but in mathematics and statistics there were two out of thirteen. In fine art there were no "excellents" out of four, even though the Scottish art colleges enjoy high reputations and more generous resource allocation than their English counterparts.

Fourth, the subject-by-subject coverage approach taken in Scotland has generally been out-of-step with the approach taken in the rest of the United Kingdom. This is by no means a criticism of the SHEFC; indeed, it is quite the reverse. The SHEFC was initially more efficient in its quality assessment activities and, especially compared to England, had the advantage of having a much smaller system to cover. In subject areas where assessments have taken place concurrently on both sides of the border, however, there has been a divergence in the proportion of "excellent" grades awarded, usually to Scotland's disadvantage. Does this truly reflect a lower quality of program or activity within Scottish higher education, or is it the result of separate procedures operating differently in the two countries? Within Scotland itself, the results do not necessarily pose a problem. However, Scottish higher education recruits a significant number of its students (currently approximately 17 percent of its undergraduates) from the rest of the United Kingdom, and because many overseas students and their sponsors see U.K. higher education as a single system, these disparate results cause considerable confusion and negative opinions about Scottish higher education.

Fifth, the relatively small number of members in the team of assessors representing each cognate area has meant that most assessors have visited a relatively high proportion of the institutions involved. In addition, the assessment activity in any one cognate area is completed within a single academic year, after which the teams are disbanded. This, coupled with the competitive climate within which quality assessments take place, means that the quality assessment process itself has not achieved much of its potential in terms of its developmental role for the benefit of the total sector. This contrasts negatively, for example, with the procedures of the former Council for National Academic Awards, which conducted the validation and review procedures for the nonuniversity higher education institutions prior to 1992.

Sixth, in certain of its annual reports on quality assessment, the SHEFC (1995) has expressed its disappointment that in general Scottish institutions' self-assessment documents have tended to overrate their own provisions. The SHEFC has used this argument to exhort institutions to be more self-critical in their self-assessments. The institutions, however, have felt that bidding up the results in self-assessments are inevitable in a highly competitive process in which the results are published. In addition, when certain cognate areas in several institutions have been self-critical and have identified weaknesses, assessors have pounced on those weaknesses and highlighted them, even when institutions have already been taking remedial action. Thus, several institutions have felt aggrieved by the process.

Seventh, the participation of assessors in the assessment of only Scottish institutions has severely restricted the extent to which they can learn from and contribute to developments in institutions throughout the United Kingdom. Indeed, given the increasing emphasis on attracting international students, the case for introducing an international dimension to quality assessment has also been growing.

Eighth, a number of institutions have expressed the view that publishing the assessment reports has reduced the value of the quality assessment activity because the reports have attempted to achieve three different and to some extent conflicting purposes. The first of these purposes has been to inform the SHEFC itself, the second has been to inform the parties who constitute "the market," and the third has been to inform the institutions themselves about what their peers think of them. The reports have been drafted by sophisticated, well-informed assessors who have read copious documentation and visited the relevant departments in the institutions concerned, meeting with senior management, teaching staff, students, support service providers, and secretarial staff. The views expressed by these assessors, who write from a relatively well-informed perspective, may be interpreted quite differently by the generally unsophisticated lay reader of a free-standing report who lacks all the supporting technical information. As a result, in an attempt to satisfy all parties, the wording of reports has often been very bland. Criticisms have frequently been toned down, for example, in an effort to avoid causing offense or to avoid other damage. Although this approach may please institutions when the reports are published, it may ultimately be of less benefit to them as a means of achieving any genuine quality enhancement.

Ninth, the new (post-1992) universities and the remaining nonuniversity higher education institutions have felt that although quality assessments initially aimed to assess "fitness for purpose," this element has become less apparent as the cycle has progressed. Increasingly, the pre-1992 universities, which had been better funded for teaching as well as funded for research, performed disproportionately well in quality assessments. As a result, the award of additional funding to help secure "excellent" ratings merely increased the resource disparity with other institutions.

Impact of Quality Assurance on Higher Education Practices in Scotland: Outcomes and Lessons Learned

A number of themes can be identified in the impact that implementation of these processes has had on higher education in Scotland, and in their implications for the future:

- Changes in the organization and communication of teaching
- Changes in teaching practices and in curricula
- Changes in quality assurance processes within institutions
- Increasing centralization within institutions

External quality assurance processes have had significant impacts on how teaching is described and communicated; this feature can be attributed to three principal "drivers." First, the frameworks associated with the quality assurance processes refer specifically to systematic organization and communication. Second, the processes themselves, in combination with the visits and the scrutiny of documentation, demand that departments be able to describe their activities effectively and clearly. Assessors have frequently placed greatest emphasis on documentation issued to students, seeing this as the "real" or operational evidence of quality. This has significantly influenced how curricula and teaching are described. Third, assessor training and the ways in which assessors operationally evaluate quality and make grading decisions reward systematic organization and communication.

A number of areas of emphasis can be identified over the period of implementation:

- *Aims and objectives.* There has been a definite trend toward making systematic statements of learning objectives and of the outcomes associated with courses of study, plus a justification of why they are considered to be appropriate.

Traditionally, many academics have described curricula exclusively in terms of subject content—that is, in terms of syllabus topics rather than in terms of student outcomes. The process of defining such aims has in many cases triggered a review and revision of content.

• *Personal transferable skills.* Both the evaluation framework and the assessors' comments have emphasized the importance of personal transferable (generic or key) skills in curriculum design, delivery, and assessment.

• *Student-centered or in-depth learning.* Approaches that promote student engagement and encourage in-depth or active learning have been encouraged, both in the evaluation framework and in assessors' comments.

• *Innovation and development of teaching practice.* Innovation in teaching methods, especially the development of methods that seek to promote in-depth learning or transferable skills, has generally been regarded as a positive thing.

• *Levels and progression.* Assessors frequently look for evidence of the progression of learning, from year to year and within programs of study, focusing in particular on assessment arrangements and criteria.

• *Links between research and teaching.* In departments that are active in research there has generally been an emphasis on ways that undergraduate students benefit from being taught in a research environment.

In some cases these trends have led to academic departments developing explicit statements of previously implicit practices. In other cases, changes in practices have occurred, partly driven by internal institutional quality assurance processes and partly triggered by the process of trying to develop explicit statements of existing practice that lead to the identification of needs or opportunities for change. These trends tend to be identified and then adopted and embedded in practices in successive years; that is, issues raised or emphasized by teams of assessors in the first year of the cycle are reported and then influence practice in the next year. This process of progressive "embedment" has been reported by Trow (1994).

The external quality assurance processes and procedures have stimulated changes in internal quality assurance practices and procedures within institutions, both in the organization and management efforts and in internal policy and procedures. Institutions have generally increased management staff resources allocated to quality assurance, both in implementing internal procedures and in supporting external assessment exercises. Staff in these situations frequently assume the role of change agents, keeping track of issues raised by external quality assurance assessors and feeding them into both institutional procedures and departmental practices. In particular, issues raised or deficiencies exposed by external assessors can lead to changes in institutional quality assurance policies and procedures. Similarly, internal academic staff, who are utilized by external agencies as assessors, can import good practices and procedures from elsewhere to their home institutions. Even allowing for the proper safeguards of confidentiality, such opportunities do represent a very valuable opportunity for faculty to have a voice in the overall assessment process and to gain insights into actual assessment practices and best practices elsewhere.

These changes can take place at various stages in the assessment cycle, but in our institution we have found that the most significant modifications generally take place during the self-assessment phase. This same pattern has been noted in wider studies, for example, in the experience in England during 1993–1995 reported by Brennan, Frederiks, and Shah (1997).

The importation and implementation of external quality assurance practices has also had the general effect of increasing the centralization of academic affairs within institutions. For example, the codification of institution-wide rules and the adoption of generic systems have become more centralized. This trend, disparagingly described as bureaucratization, has been discussed by a number of authors, including Kogan (1996) and Bauer and Henkel (1996).

Review of Quality Assessment Efforts and the Future Outlook

The criticisms of the SHEFC's quality assurance program listed earlier suggest that whatever its achievements are, there might be ways of achieving greater benefit for the Scottish higher education sector as a whole. Increasingly aware of this view, the SHEFC in 1995 instigated a major review of its quality assessment procedures that largely accepted the criticisms and suggestions put forward by the institutions (Scottish Higher Education Funding Council-Committee of Scottish Higher Education Principals, 1996). There was, however, one major and crucial exception. The review did not endorse the unanimous proposal by the institutions that quality assessments should no longer be conducted separately in Scotland, and that Scottish institutions should participate in a single U.K. quality assessment system. Such an approach would not only have the advantage of broadening the horizons of quality assessment but would also offer a broader scope for better coordination with quality audits that are already conducted throughout the United Kingdom by the HEQC.

The new QAAHE, however, established in 1997 as a result of a U.K. review (Higher Education Funding Council for England–Committee of Vice Chancellors and Principals, 1996), was asked not only to absorb the functions of the HEQC but also to devise a new, all-encompassing U.K. approach to quality assessment. Under considerable pressure, both politically and from the institutions, the SHEFC reluctantly agreed not to start a second cycle of separate assessments, and to join the new U.K. program. In the meantime, however, the emerging methodology for the U.K. approach has placed increasing importance on the coalescing of the separate quality audit and quality assessment into a single set of procedures (Quality Assurance Agency for Higher Education, 1998). This viewpoint has been welcomed by institutions that hope that the bureaucratic demands of two separate but sometimes overlapping activities might be reduced and that the new approach will place greater emphasis on an institution-wide audit than on subject-by-subject assessments. The SHEFC, in particular, however, argues that it needs quality assessment information at the subject level in order to meet its statutory obligations and the political imperative of linking funding allocations to quality ratings. The development and introduction of the new procedures will be watched with great interest, and it is hoped that even if the previous misgivings can be overcome, the beneficial effects of quality assurance in changing the teaching and learning culture will be maintained under the future arrangements.

References

Bauer, M., and Henkel, M. *Responses of Academe to Quality Reforms in Higher Education: A Comparative Study of England and Sweden.* Paper presented at the eighteenth annual European Association of Institutional Research (EAIR) Forum, Budapest, Hungary, Aug. 1996.

Brennan, J., Frederiks, M., and Shah, T. *Improving the Quality of Education: The Impact of Quality Assessment on Institutions.* London: Quality Support Center, 1997.

Entwistle, N. "The Use of Research on Student Learning in Quality Assessment." In G. Gibbs (ed.), *Improving Student Learning Through Assessment and Evaluation.* Oxford, U.K.: Oxford Center for Staff Development, 1995.

Higher Education Quality Council. *Learning from Audit.* London: Higher Education Quality Council, 1994.

Higher Education Quality Council. *Learning from Audit 2.* London: Higher Education Quality Council, 1996.

Higher Education Funding Council For England–Committee of Vice Chancellors and Principals. *Joint Planning Group for Quality Assurance in Higher Education: Final Report.* London: Higher Education Funding Council For England–Committee of Vice Chancellors and Principals, 1996.

Kogan, M. *Academics and Administrators in Higher Education.* Paper presented at the Consortium of Higher Education Researchers (CHER) Conference, Turku, Finland, June 1996.

Quality Assurance Agency for Higher Education. "Consultation Issue." [http://www.niss.ac.uk/education/qaa/pub98/hq_1_3.html]. Accessed Mar. 1998.

Scottish Higher Education Funding Council. *Quality Assessment Annual Report 1993–94.* Edinburgh: Scottish Higher Education Funding Council, 1995.

Scottish Higher Education Funding Council. *Quality Assessment Assessors Handbook.* Edinburgh: Scottish Higher Education Funding Council, 1993a.

Scottish Higher Education Funding Council. *Quality Assessment Assessors Handbook.* Annexe QA/1. Edinburgh: Scottish Higher Education Funding Council, 1993b.

Scottish Higher Education Funding Council–Committee of Scottish Higher Education Principals. *Joint Review Group on Quality Assessment.* Edinburgh: Scottish Higher Education Funding Council, 1996.

Trow, M. *Managerialism and the Academic Profession: Quality and Control.* Quality Support Center Higher Education Report no. 2. London: Quality Support Center/Open University Press, 1994.

University of Dundee. "Mission Statement." [http://www.dundee.ac.uk/mission.htm]. Accessed Aug. 6, 1998..

CHRIS CARTER *is former deputy principal at the University of Dundee, Scotland.*

ALAN DAVIDSON *is the quality advisory officer at the University of Dundee, Scotland.*

*Entrepreneurial universities—nontraditional institutions that provide
instructional services in alternative formats at multiple locations—
face a variety of challenges as they attempt to incorporate quality
assurance and improvement strategies. This chapter reviews the
development of these institutions, the resistance they face within
academe, and the processes they use to satisfy regulatory bodies,
inform constituencies, and improve organizational processes.*

Quality Assurance in the Entrepreneurial University

John E. Neal

In the multicolored tapestry of academia a new colored strand has appeared—
different but not yet distinct enough to permit clear identification—the "entrepreneurial" university. Over the past twenty-five years, a number of these
institutions have evolved, shifted, or stumbled into an organizational structure
that is more strategic and businesslike than the traditional academy of scholars. This movement has produced a variety of unique institutions, yet they
speak, act, and react in very similar ways. Descriptions of how these universities operate sound like descriptions of Fortune 500 companies: they build
strategic visions based on scans of the competitive environment; they refer to
market niches, client profiles, and delivery systems, while insisting on curricular integrity and relevance, instructional quality, and student satisfaction.
These institutions have expanded higher education's attention to poorly served
segments of society—especially adult learners and people who are not geo-
graphically close to a college or university—while pushing the envelope of distance learning, the use of instructional technology, and the connection of
coursework to career and lifelong learning. At the same time, these institutions
have also challenged traditional notions of academic rigor and quality.

To many, if not most, in the traditional higher education community, the
idea of an entrepreneurial university is an oxymoron. To expand the notion to
a discussion of quality assurance within the entrepreneurial university would
therefore be a waste of time. This chapter challenges these biases by examining aspects of the entrepreneurial movement in higher education and its relationship to traditional conceptions of quality, and it explores the academy's
ability to innovate while addressing issues of accountability and integrity.

New Directions for Institutional Research, no. 99, Fall 1998 © Jossey-Bass Publishers

The chapter's title suggests that the entrepreneurial segment of higher education is clearly defined and that its institutions are readily identified and correctly categorized—but they are not. Given this open definition and lack of firm boundary, this chapter explores traits or themes in institutions that appear to be entrepreneurial, and it presents examples from specific institutions that illustrate issues common to many institutions. These issues and their implications for quality assurance will have application to a wider number of institutions as certain environmental factors and economic pressures increase. Just as *marketing* once was a disparaged term at any respectable university, so the developments discussed here will be imitated and absorbed by other institutions in the new millennium—not out of admiration but out of necessity.

The chapter explores the following questions: What does it mean to be entrepreneurial? What is an entrepreneurial university? Are the concepts of quality and entrepreneurship contradictory in this context? What are the primary indicators of quality for this type of endeavor? Do they differ from those for other types of institutions? How does culture affect this phenomenon? Is the entrepreneurial university a distinctly American institution? What models of quality assurance exist for this segment of higher education?

Defining Entrepreneurship

As with most emerging organizational trends, the coining and frequent use of a term—particularly jargon or a buzzword—often precede its thoughtful definition and utilization. The label *entrepreneurial* may suggest pejoratively a university characterized by aggressiveness, risk taking, and an emphasis on quick return on investment. An examination of scholarship on entrepreneurship suggests that the term may be difficult to define. Furthermore, superficial bias against the application of the concept to higher education may miss deeper concepts that challenge traditional methods of university administration, leadership, and delivery of services.

The Ewing Marion Kauffman Foundation, a national leader in research on entrepreneurship, operates the Center for Entrepreneurial Leadership to encourage and enable entrepreneurship in five categories: the economy, public policy, the education system, inner cities and communities, and the not-for-profit sector. The foundation asserts that not-for-profit leaders require just as much, if not more, entrepreneurial skill as their for-profit counterparts (Ewing Marion Kauffman Foundation, 1997). By training the leaders of not-for-profits, they hope to help identify innovative ways to advance the social missions of these organizations. As one might expect from an outcomes-oriented institution, however, the foundation's materials concentrate on what an entrepreneur does rather than on defining the term.

Bygrave and Hofer (1991) contend that the development of a theoretical foundation remains a major challenge in the field of entrepreneurship. They assert that no general agreement exists among scholars on either a general definition of the term or on a clear characterization of the entrepreneurial process.

In the absence of clear consensus on these issues, a number of articles suggest definitions of the nature and process of entrepreneurship.

Stevenson and Gumpert (1985) contend that definitions of entrepreneurship by managers (to be innovative, flexible, dynamic, risk taking, creative, and growth oriented) and in the popular press (to start and operate new ventures) are not precise or prescriptive enough to be of help to aspiring entrepreneurs. They suggest viewing entrepreneurship as a range of behavior, differentiating it from that of the typical administrator. When making decisions, administrators and entrepreneurs pursue a different set of questions. Administrators ask the following (p. 86): What resources do I control? What structure determines our organization's relationship to its market? How can I minimize the impact of others on my ability to perform? What opportunity is appropriate?

The entrepreneur asks the following (p. 87): Where is the opportunity? How do I capitalize on it? What resources do I need? How do I gain control over them? What structure is best?

Stevenson and Gumpert further specify key characteristics for these two approaches (entrepreneurial and administrative), differentiating them on the five critical dimensions listed in Table 6.1.

Utilizing Stevenson and Gumpert's descriptive framework of management cultures, an entrepreneurial university would be characterized by the following qualities:

A focus on environmental changes in technology, the economy, social values, and regulations that would open windows of opportunity

An action orientation within narrow decision windows utilizing input from a limited number of constituencies, based on an acceptance of reasonable risks

A realization of the lack of predictable resources, combined with an emphasis on efficient and appropriate use of resources

Table 6.1. Key Characteristics of the Entrepreneurial and Administrative Approaches

Critical Dimensions	Entrepreneurial	Administrative
Strategic orientation	Driven by perception of opportunity	Driven by controlled resources
Commitment to seize opportunities	Revolutionary, with short duration	Evolutionary, with long duration
Commitment of resources	Many stages, with minimal exposure at each stage	A single stage, with complete commitment from decision
Control of resources	Episodic use or rent of required resources	Ownership or employment of required resources
Management structure	Flat, with multiple informal networks	Hierarchy

Source: Compiled from Stevenson and Gumpert, 1985, p. 89.

A distinction between the use and the acquisition of required resources (cap-
   ital and human) based on considerations of specialization, flexibility, potential for obsolescence, and resource life
An ability to organize and reorganize decision-making structures based on
   external and internal opportunities

   An entrepreneurial culture differs widely from the culture of an administra-
tively focused university, which would be characterized by the following elements:

Formal planning systems and the fulfillment of performance criteria
Reduction or elimination of risk in decision making through consultation with
   multiple constituencies and the development of negotiated strategic plans
Budgeting systems based on predictable and controlled resources, designed to
   reward fulfillment of performance goals and to encourage continuity of management and personnel
Acquisition and coordination of resources to increase organizational status and
   power
Clearly delineated structures with defined roles, responsibilities, and authority for participants

   I propose the following working definition of an entrepreneurial university: an institution focused on nontraditional students (predominantly adult,
part-time) that emphasizes the delivery of instructional services (as opposed
to research or community outreach activities) in alternative formats (time,
place, or technology) at multiple locations (including across state lines and
national borders). The leadership style within this type of institution would
emphasize aggressive yet planned growth and expansion, openness to a wide
range of partnerships and collaborative agreements, and the leasing of key
resources (including faculty and facilities) to minimize administrative overhead
and maximize future flexibility. The essence of entrepreneurship, then, seems
to be a willingness to move out of traditional delivery structures—campuses
and classrooms—and to seek new audiences and serve new constituencies
through collaborations.

The Entrepreneurial University

Can Stevenson and Gumpert's framework be used to identify specific entrepreneurial organizations, units, or even trends in higher education? Halal
(1997) identifies a trend in which increased enterprise and democracy are creating a "new management for the information age" (p. 3). Similar to the health
care industry, which is criticized for excessive bureaucracy and mediocre service, higher education faces public scrutiny and complaints regarding rising
tuition, the quality of instruction, the connection of study to employment, the
shelf life of knowledge in a rapidly changing world, and the frustrations of
dealing with a well-entrenched hierarchy.

The traditional campus and classroom model served universities well in the past, because it managed routine tasks effectively in a stable environment. In light of the accelerating knowledge revolution, Halal (1997) considers the traditional system so outdated that it no longer fulfills the demands of a dynamic modern university. In an attempt to include all possible constituencies in as many decisions and deliberations as possible, traditional universities, particularly public ones, have become so entrenched in bureaucracy that they often strangle all attempts to innovate or deviate from the status quo (Mac-Taggart and Associates, 1998). Meanwhile, other types of institutions have turned their organizations into fluid collections of small entrepreneurial units, creating a constellation of "internal markets" connected by informal networks (Halal, 1997, p. 4).

Halal applies these principles to traditional universities, suggesting that departments become self-supporting units, or pockets of entrepreneurship, operating on an agreed-upon portion of the revenue they generate. Funding levels may also reflect performance against institutional measures of key activities or outcomes. Departments held accountable for their performance should then be free to manage their own operations. Lundquist (1996) observes a linking of resource allocation and performance at a number of traditional universities, such as the University of Michigan, Indiana University, the University of Southern California, and the University of Pennsylvania; the latter employs a budgeting system emphasizing "each tub on its own bottom," which further encourages entrepreneurship. These institutions utilize strategic planning, activity-based accounting, and other management tools to help academic units take greater responsibility for their expenses and their revenues, and reward or punish consequences based on success and failure.

Bollag (1997) reports on a growing entrepreneurial climate throughout European higher education as declining government funding fails to keep pace with growing enrollments. To generate additional institutional funds needed to grow or sustain current activities, universities are performing applied research for business and industry, while also providing continuing education programs for businesses and government agencies. In most European higher education systems, reductions in state funding have been accompanied by the granting of increased institutional autonomy and flexibility—which encourages institutions to be more market driven.

Clark (1997) documents the efforts of five European universities (University of Warwick, University of Twente, University of Strathclyde, Chalmers University of Technology, and the University of Joensuu) to become more proactive and entrepreneurial over a ten- to fifteen-year period. His study identifies five common elements, or "pathways to transformation," in creating a proactive, adaptive, and effective institution:

1. *A strengthened steering core:* A "centralized decentralization" in which strong personal leadership gives way to collegial groups, combined with stronger line authority.

2. *An enhanced developmental periphery:* Outreach administrative units that promote contracted services and consultancies for the university.
3. *A diversified funding base:* While ambition encourages diversification, competition demands it.
4. *A stimulated academic heartland:* Because entrepreneurial activity will spread unevenly among traditional academic departments, the university must prepare for a period of transition, a schizophrenic state, that is entrepreneurial on one side and traditional on the other.
5. *The entrepreneurial culture:* A need to identify key organizational ideas and beliefs and relate them to structures that support processes of change.

Clark traces the current age of turmoil within higher education to one issue: demands on universities have outrun their capacities to respond. These demands include greater and broader access to higher education, a greater number of highly trained and specialized occupations, higher expectations from larger numbers of constituencies, and the tendency of the growth of knowledge to outrun resources. Clark contends that the entrepreneurial response gives universities greater capacities to redefine their reach by including more useful knowledge, moving more flexibly over time from one program emphasis to another, and building an organizational identity and focus. (See Chapter Two in this volume, on the Netherlands, by Peter Maassen.)

Daniel (1996) provides a detailed examination of a unique segment of higher education—the *mega-university*—which uncovers and capitalizes on issues of growing interest and concern for higher education in general and the entrepreneurial university in particular. He defines the mega-university as an institution that provides degree-level courses primarily through distance learning technologies to more than one hundred thousand active students. According to Daniel, these mega-universities battle traditional measures of institutional reputation and quality, such as institutional age, wealth, and exclusiveness of student admission. In addition, they confront long-standing perceptions correlating low instructional quality with large enrollments, as well as the perennially low status of correspondence study. Britain's Open University provides an example of a mega-university institution that has freed itself from low status to receive excellent ratings in the U.K. quality assessment. Daniel outlines the ingredients of their success: good course materials; tutorial and regional support networks; a mixture of instructional delivery systems that incorporate technology; significant graduation rates; appropriate staffing levels; vibrant research activity; and a culture that promotes a sense of academic community.

On the American front, what trends are shaping the development of entrepreneurial universities? Are there examples of institutions that utilize varying degrees of entrepreneurship in the design, development, and delivery of postsecondary instruction in the United States? The prescience of some visionary authors suggests that future learning modes will require more entrepreneurial efforts. Norris (1998) lists four adjectives that describe the type of learning that will succeed in the emerging "knowledge age": perpetual, distributed, interactive, and collaborative. He contends that institutions that address these issues will experience substantial growth in the twenty-first century, in spite of intense competition. Those that ignore these aspects of learning will lose market share to new entrepreneurial competitors and alternative methods of delivery. Norris envisions a segmentation of the higher education market, based on distributed learning, evolving from traditional to semitraditional to nontraditional approaches in delivering both undergraduate and graduate programs. This shift from traditional to semitraditional and nontraditional instruction can be charted in the higher education literature and even within the popular press.

Raphael and Tobias (1997) highlight the emergence of nontraditional institutions in the Arizona teacher education market. In addition to discussing the University of Phoenix (which will receive more attention shortly), the article explores the activities of Chapman University and Ottawa University in the delivery of teacher certification programs. Chapman (founded in 1861 and based in Orange, California) and Ottawa (founded in Ottawa, Kansas in 1865) represent nonprofit, private, multisite institutions operating both traditional residential campuses and adult satellite centers across the United States (and in Ottawa's case, in the Pacific Rim). The relative success of these distributed institutions has resulted in increased coverage by the popular press and increased scrutiny from traditional counterparts. In 1996, Ottawa University ranked second only to Arizona State University in the number of teachers it prepared for Arizona certification (p. 48). Although these nontraditional programs are higher priced than public institutions because they are unsubsidized, they have experienced substantial enrollment growth. One major influence in the growth of these nontraditional programs over traditional, public offerings—despite the high prices of the nontraditional programs—is that "students are considered customers, or clients, and are treated differently from undergraduate or graduate students at traditional universities, where 'customer' is a bad word and students often come low on the priority list" (p. 47). Such a customer-oriented philosophy represents the very basis of a successful quality assurance program in academe.

The *Chronicle of Higher Education* (Rubin, 1997) describes Webster University's entrepreneurial drive to become a global university. This globalization trend is a growing feature of most entrepreneurial institutions. Rather than signing agreements with foreign institutions for faculty and student exchange, or offering business and English language courses for foreign nationals, Webster operates its own campuses and customized courses in five countries, with plans for worldwide expansion. These campuses serve local students, as well as students from other countries and from its home campus in St. Louis.

Recent efforts by Western Governors University (WGU) to create a "virtual university" raise a number of challenges that would be faced by any nontraditional institution interested in a significant instructional presence on the Internet or other technology-based delivery system. Incorporated as a private, nonprofit institution, WGU created a fourteen-member board of trustees and currently consists of twenty-one colleges and corporations that will provide coursework via computer or other technology (Blumenstyk, 1998). WGU will pursue a three-part mission: it will serve as an electronic clearinghouse for distance-learning courses provided by existing colleges or companies; it will provide training programs to corporate employees; and it will award degrees and certificates in academic and technical fields through mastery of specified competencies (Leavitt, 1996). University officials realize that courses and programs are available from a wide variety of sources, such as individual institutions or other ventures, such as the IBM Global Campus (Oblinger, 1996), the Southern Regional Electronic Campus, and the California Virtual University. No consistent standard or protocol for quality assurance exists at present, however, for such providers of educational services. In light of these concerns about quality, WGU faces a number of hurdles, including initial accreditation, while convincing skeptics of the viability of its plans for on-line library access and competency-based degrees, without its own distinct, core faculty (Blumenstyk, 1998).

As WGU and other collaborative endeavors attempt to build a virtual educational organization, a number of existing institutions offer degree programs via the Internet and other distance learning technologies. These programs vary from those with minimal residency requirements at the home campus or a branch campus to degrees available entirely over the Internet. Stapleton (1998) ranked twenty-five of the best such programs for *TechWeek*, emphasizing the importance of accreditation to ensure program quality. The list includes both foreign institutions—the universities of Durham, London, Wales, Waterloo, and Henley—as well as American universities—Syracuse, Idaho, Fielding, Norwich, and Ottawa. Gubernick and Ebeling (1997) report that 55 percent of American universities have courses available on-line, and they list their own rankings of top programs, including Carnegie Mellon, Duke, Nova Southeastern, Thomas Edison, and the University of Phoenix.

Although a number of programs, departments, and institutions display entrepreneurial tendencies, perhaps no other institution has gained as much notoriety in the academy, the business community, and the press as the University of Phoenix. For many people, the University of Phoenix sets the standard for entrepreneurial higher education. For others, it represents all that is flawed with the entrepreneurial model. In 1997, the Apollo Group, of which the University of Phoenix is the largest and most profitable subsidiary, reported net revenues of $283.5 million (Strosnider, 1998). John Sperling, the University's founder, president, and chairman, has guided the institution's growth from its inception in 1974 to ninety-eight campuses in thirty-one states and an enrollment of more than fifty-five thousand students (Fischetti and others, 1998). Sperling jokes that while other institutions pound the pavement for donations and to build an endowment, Phoenix, as a for-profit corporation, has Wall Street as its endowment (Strosnider, 1997). Originally dubbed "McEducation" by an accreditor (Strosnider, 1997, p. A32), the University of Phoenix has been accredited by the North Central Association since 1978 and provides contracted services to eighteen traditional colleges for Phoenix-style adult education programs.

An examination of current trends in higher education leads to questioning of the fundamental differences between traditional universities and entrepreneurial ones. The facts listed in this chapter suggest that entrepreneurship may be a continuum, with committed traditionalists on one side and pure entrepreneurs on the other. Most universities are not as entrepreneurial as Phoenix, WGU, or Open University but instead are a mixture of entrepreneurial and administrative. Many have become predominantly entrepreneurial, such as Webster, Ottawa, and Chapman, while a host of other institutions, including traditional models, experiment and incorporate entrepreneurial aspects in order to fuel growth, change, and responsiveness to environmental opportunities—preferably in ways that are consistent with their mission and goals.

Quality Versus Entrepreneurship?

For some, this recounting of entrepreneurial trends and institutional activity provides evidence of a sea change in higher education—a fundamental shift in the way universities must learn to do business if they are to survive and thrive in the next century. For others, these activities provide a clarion wake-up call that the academy has lost its way, has forsaken its fundamental purpose and distinctive character to pursue fame and fortune. In both groups, the critical issue remains quality—that is, regardless of the particular approach or methodology, any entrepreneurial university must find coherent and persuasive ways of measuring, documenting, and ensuring the quality of its programs in order to build credibility and show accountability to its key constituencies, both within the academy and among external groups.

The process of building credibility within the traditional higher education community will be difficult for entrepreneurial institutions. Even when attempting to discuss objectively the current trends and activities of these nontraditional programs and institutions, traditional academics reveal a fundamental bias that such programs and institutions do not provide "real" higher education, or certainly not a "high quality" educational experience. Consider the following examples: *Change* magazine's listing of "America's higher education leaders" included John Sperling, president of the University of Phoenix, but listed him as an "external influencer" (Munitz and Breneman, 1998, p. 18). While noting his extraordinary financial success, the authors characterize his model as "all-too-full of shortcuts" (p. 18). Raphael and Tobias's (1997) discussion of nontraditional institutions and teacher education programs in Arizona seems more an exposé than a balanced treatment of the phenomenon. They view proprietary schools (such as Phoenix) as motivated solely by profits, and "non-profit niche-seekers" (p. 48) such as Ottawa and Chapman as driven by money rather than mission. Even *The New Yorker* pejoratively entitled its largely complimentary treatment of Phoenix (and Ottawa) "Drive-Thru U" (Traub, 1997).

Quality Assurance

In the face of these preconceived notions (or bad experiences), are there any quality assurance initiatives appropriate for the entrepreneurial sector that may help minimize such concerns and criticisms while building credibility among external partners? Bogue (1993, and Chapter One of this volume) contends that conventional elitist assumptions about academic quality perpetuate the belief that only a few institutions can be of high quality and that they are expensive, large, selective, and nationally recognized. High academic quality does not come through imitation of a few elite institutions, however, but by discovering, defining, and fulfilling an institution's own unique promise and distinction. Bogue provides a definition of such quality as institutional "conformance to mission specification and goal achievement—within publicly accepted standards of accountability and integrity" (1993, p. 290). The entrepreneurial university can develop, define, measure, and disseminate the quality of its efforts using such a definition.

Tucker (1997) discusses the varied responses to quality assessment throughout higher education and recommends the creation of a coherent family of definitions of quality to inform policy discussions and institutional planning and procedures. He also recommends the development of common criteria for evaluating various definitions of quality. In spite of the difficulties faced in achieving effective quality assessment, Tucker considers three steps as essential to further progress: constituent groups must clarify their definitions of quality and place them within a broader context of public discussion; issues and definitions must be made explicit, subjected to public discussion, and given legitimacy; and a timetable for results must be set.

A review of activities within the entrepreneurial segment of higher education using Bogue's principles outlined in Chapter One in this volume suggests that these universities must envision quality as both fulfilling their missions and adding value to the participant, within broadly established standards of quality. Bogue's quality principles provide a useful framework for identifying new quality assurance activities for nontraditional institutions and for relating them to key institutional decisions that improve processes and performance. The design of a quality mechanism for the entrepreneurial institution must, at minimum, do the following: give evidence of performance and improvement; show a connection between evidence and decision making; demonstrate the mechanism's programmatic relationship to mission fulfillment; facilitate the creation of efficient and effective systems; link quality assurance to teaching and learning; and submit to external standards and judgments.

Institutions within the entrepreneurial sector would argue that effective quality assurance and improvement processes are perhaps more vital for the survival and future success of such institutions than they are for traditional institutions. Consider the many quality control mechanisms that entrepreneurial institutions currently employ, such as teacher evaluation and program review mechanisms, review of academic coursework, student evaluations of courses and instructors, faculty review procedures, student assessment throughout their programs of study, employer assessments of graduates and programs, and alumni satisfaction surveys. All provide immediate feedback on the quality of educational offerings while providing information for future program development and strengthening student support services. Entrepreneurs would also contend that the fulfillment of organizational mission must include the fulfillment of student and employer expectations—customer satisfaction in quality assurance terms—or students may choose an entrepreneurial competitor or a less expensive traditional program.

Those who are wary of the entrepreneurial phenomenon would push for stricter regulation, control, and monitoring of these institutions. For them, the accreditation process or program certification imposes necessary minimum standards and protects consumers of the educational product. Perhaps both views represent valid concerns as this sector grows. As entrepreneurial universities strive for acceptance and for their own sense of excellence and success, progressive regulatory bodies struggle for ways to enforce necessary controls without stifling individuality and innovation.

Quality Models

As with innovative organizations in business and industry that deal with "industrial espionage," entrepreneurial universities are permeated by the desire to retain competitive advantage and the corresponding secrets of success. Institutional paranoia results from repeated experiences in developing innovative programs or processes, enduring ridicule and scorn from traditional institutions, and enjoying limited success, then watching traditional institutions emulate, improve, and adopt the very same model, ultimately resulting in new competition from one's harshest critics. These experiences make entrepreneurial institutions skittish about submitting to external review still controlled by traditional institutions, and about widespread dissemination of successful organizational processes and procedures.

In spite of these tendencies to conceal their trade secrets, most entrepreneurial institutions operate their quality control processes in quite similar ways, with some understandable differences that result from institutional mission and educational philosophy. The similarities usually result from constraints placed on the institutions by external review entities.

Within the important realm of academic program quality, for instance, most entrepreneurial universities place the responsibility for curricular issues in the hands of full-time faculty. The University of Phoenix, for example, maintains a corps of twenty-six faculty members to design course syllabi and make textbook selections for each course, regardless of its location. Part-time instructors are hired to communicate the predesigned content and fulfill the planned objectives of the course. Extensive student testing validates course and program outcomes (Fischetti and others, 1998).

Webster University, conversely, combines the culture of a traditional campus faculty with part-time or adjunct instructors at its satellite campuses. Candidates for part-time appointments are reviewed by corresponding academic departments at the main campus and syllabi are standardized by faculty curriculum committees, but adjunct instructors are permitted and even expected to incorporate their own professional experience and academic preparation into the course content. This allows for wider variation in the content and outcomes of courses than found in the Phoenix model.

Ottawa University decentralizes its faculty control of academic content by hiring full-time faculty at each of its regional centers as well as at its residential campus. Although the design of degree programs is reviewed by a central university academic council assembled from its various centers, the syllabi and content of each course remain the responsibility of the full-time faculty at each center. Regular team assessments of academic programs across all centers involve faculty from every location, as well as external participants from other universities, businesses, and organizations. These reviews ensure consistency in design and desired outcomes without imposing a level of homogeneity that disregards local needs and culture.

Some entrepreneurial institutions have developed and published detailed handbooks outlining their quality assurance approaches. These handbooks have largely resulted from activities to satisfy regulatory bodies, such as the self-study process for U.S. accreditation.

At the institutional level, the U.K.'s Open University has developed an extensive quality assurance process in response to the quality assessment initiative of the Higher Education Funding Council for England (HEFCE). O'Shea, Bearman, and Downes (1997) confirm from their experiences with HEFCE that any external assessment process must be flexible enough to permit diversity of institutional mission. Although regulatory bodies and funding councils would not disagree with this statement, they would find it difficult to put into practice with nontraditional institutions, because the pool of reviewers largely comes from more traditional organizations. For instance, an evaluation of teaching quality on a traditional campus would typically include classroom observation. This would be difficult, if not impossible, for nontraditional institutions that offer instruction through distance-learning approaches. The Open University accepted the challenge of undergoing external assessment by helping HEFCE evaluate its conceptions of quality in all dimensions of institutional life while also being vulnerable to misunderstanding by the traditional university community. Taking initiative in this endeavor broadened HEFCE's concept of quality and increased recognition of the Open University as a high-quality university.

The Open University's formal guide to quality assurance (1997) outlines the aim of this process (p. 1): "to embed quality assurance in organizational structures, staff responsibilities and high level process design, but within guidelines, allow for a range of practices and mechanisms in different academic and administrative units, to suit different cultural and local needs. . . . Our approach to quality assurance focuses on the development of staff to enable them to carry out their jobs well, learn from feedback, and contribute to a continuous process of improvement. New processes, methods and documentation are constantly being developed."

Responsibility for this process rests with the pro-vice-chancellor (vice president) for quality assurance and research. This senior-level position oversees a number of institutional components related to quality:

Quality Assurance Panel: chaired by the vice-chancellor (president) of the university and composed of senior officials from across the institution

Institute of Educational Technology: an academic research unit specializing in educational technology and quality assurance services to university units

Quality Support Center: a freestanding and self-financed unit providing consultancy on quality improvement to higher education institutions

Quality Assurance Groups: established by individual units to identify quality-related issues

Staff Development Committee: coordinates with the pro-vice-chancellor's development programs for new and continuing staff in light of unit plans and quality assurance objectives

Monitoring and Feedback Steering Group: coordinates the collection of feedback data from students and faculty to inform course design, development, and delivery, as well as student support services

Regional Academic Services: provides coordination of services to thirteen regional centers, including quality assurance activities at the regional level

The university pursues quality assessment for the purpose of improving its understanding of strengths and weaknesses in teaching, student services, student learning, and outcomes. Assessment occurs through four avenues: feedback on teaching and course quality; performance indicators on teaching, learning, and student support; evaluation of institutional performance in strategic policymaking and action; and issue-specific inquiries based on unpredictable needs, usually at the unit level.

While working with the HEFCE, the Open University continually had to remind external assessors of fundamental differences in its process of student admission, of the role of face-to-face communication, of the development of integrated teaching and learning materials rather than textbooks, and of the importance of student assessment as a teaching and learning tool. These collaborative discussions helped the university prepare for assessment visits and resulted in an improvement in its institutional rating from satisfactory to excellent (O'Shea, Bearman, and Downes, 1997).

The Open University experience illustrates the dual benefit of external review: the nontraditional institution receives an independent audit of its activities to assure minimum quality standards and to provide assurances to potential and current consumers of their services, while review agencies broaden their understanding of alternative approaches to educational delivery while expanding the number of approaches and mechanisms that are available for quality assessment. In the United States and the United Kingdom, accreditation and assessment mechanisms have a long history, yet they have focused primarily on national or regional activities (Global Alliance for Transnational Education, 1997). In 1991, the Center for Quality Assurance in International Education began as a nonprofit, collaborative activity of various U.S. higher education associations and accrediting bodies. The center focused discussion on issues of quality related to the international mobility of students, scholars, and professionals; on international linkages; and on the credentialing and recognition of programs that cross national borders. It also provided an ongoing comparative study of national quality assurance initiatives to improve national efforts and promote mobility between national systems.

One outcome of the center's activities was the creation of the Global Alliance for Transnational Education (GATE), for which the center serves as secretariat (Global Alliance for Transnational Education, 1997). GATE has developed a code of good practice for institutions offering higher education across national borders; it holds annual meetings to discuss issues of access and quality (the 1998 meeting was held in conjunction with UNESCO and OECD in Paris). It is developing a database of credit-bearing transnational educational offerings worldwide, and it provides a process of certification to validate an institution's adherence to the principles of good practice. To date, two universities have successfully completed the certification process (Rubin, 1997). Monash University, Australia's largest university, operates twenty programs serving two thousand students in Hong Kong, Malaysia, and Singapore. International University provides courses worldwide via the Internet and is a division of Jones International Ltd., a telecommunications company that also operates Mind Extension University through cable television.

The GATE certification program resembles the U.S. accreditation process in many ways. The program begins with an institutional self-study, followed by a team visit by alliance members to the home campus and to the institution's overseas sites. The team writes and submits a report to the alliance's board of directors, which votes on final institutional certification (Global Alliance for Transnational Education, 1997). The certification principles include the following quality goals that an institution must address in its self-study (pp. 31–46):

Transnational courses must be guided by goals and objectives that are understood by participants who enroll in them and must fit appropriately within the provider's mission and expertise.

Students receiving education and credentials through transnational courses must be assured by the provider that these courses have been approved by the provider and meet its criteria for educational quality, and that the same standards are applied regardless of the place or manner in which the courses are provided.

Transnational courses must comply with all appropriate laws and approvals of the host country.

Participants in transnational courses must be treated equitably and ethically. In particular, all pertinent information must be disclosed to the participants, and each participant must hold full student status or its equivalent with the provider organization.

The provider organization must have a sufficient number of fully qualified people engaged in providing the transnational courses, and their activities must be supervised and regularly evaluated as a normal activity of the provider.

The provider organization must ensure an adequate learning environment and resources for the transnational courses, and it must provide assurances that adequate resources will continue to be available until all obligations to enrolled participants are fulfilled.

Transnational courses must be pedagogically sound with respect to the methods of teaching and to the nature and needs of the learners.

The provider organization must ensure that students are provided with adequate support services to maximize the potential benefit they receive from the transnational courses.

Transnational courses must be regularly and appropriately evaluated as a normal part of the provider organization's activities, with the results of the evaluations being used to improve these courses.

Where third parties such as agents or collaborating institutions are involved, explicit written agreements must cover their roles, expectations, and obligations.

GATE's certification period lasts usually five years from the date of the review team's visit.

Conclusion

Quality assurance in the entrepreneurial university requires an openness on the part of all participants. Those within nontraditional institutions must accept more vulnerability within this highly competitive sector by revealing strengths, weaknesses, and processes to various public constituencies. Rather than fearing the loss of competitive advantage, entrepreneurial universities should welcome the opportunity to lead and participate in broader discussions of quality to build credibility, influence, and acceptance within the broader sphere of higher education policy both nationally and internationally. Those within the traditional academy should suspend their biases on the nature and function of higher education—as well as their traditional narrow notions of quality—in order to discuss fairly the role and value of entrepreneurial universities. In fact, broader participation and open discussion may provide traditional institutions with opportunities to incorporate entrepreneurial aspects into their own programs while providing alternative processes—both innovative and traditional—by which entrepreneurial universities may expand their quality improvement and assurance activities. The ability to suspend condemnation of the emerging entrepreneurial sector is well articulated by Robert Reich (1998, p. 67), former U.S. Secretary of Labor:

> I am not persuaded that the trend toward academic entrepreneurship compromises the capacity of universities to 'speak the truth to power.' If administrators articulate clear and compelling visions for their institutions, lack of direct financial control need not hobble the core intellectual mission. In fact, a looser and more entrepreneurial structure may invite a more lively and robust intellectual

life than could be contained within traditional lines of university authority. . . . Capitalism and intellectual freedom are not the same thing. But they are not opposites.

With these caveats, the future and the quality of the entrepreneurial university look bright.

References

Blumenstyk, G. "Western Governors U. Takes Shape as a New Model for Higher Education." *Chronicle of Higher Education,* Feb. 6, 1998, p. A21.

Bogue, E. G. "Defining, Assessing, and Nurturing Quality." In R. T. Ingram (ed.), *Governing Public Colleges and Universities: A Handbook for Trustees, Chief Executives, and Other Campus Leaders.* San Francisco: Jossey-Bass, 1993.

Bollag, B. "Higher Education in Europe Moves Away from State Control." *The Chronicle of Higher Education,* Nov. 7, 1997, pp. A47–A48.

Bygrave, W. D., and Hofer, C. W. "Theorizing About Entrepreneurship." *Entrepreneurship Theory and Practice,* Winter 1991, pp. 1–10.

Clark, B. R. *The Entrepreneurial University: Demand and Response.* Paper presented at the nineteenth annual European Association of Institutional Research (EAIR) Forum, Warwick, United Kingdom, Aug. 1997.

Daniel, J. S. *Mega-Universities and Knowledge Media.* London: Kegan Paul, 1996.

Ewing Marion Kauffman Foundation. *Annual Report.* Kansas City, Mo.: Ewing Marion Kauffman Foundation, 1997.

Fischetti, M., Anderson, J., Watrous, M., Tanz, J., and Gwynne, P. "Gas, Food, Lodging . . . Education?" *University Business,* Mar./Apr. 1998, pp. 44–51.

Global Alliance for Transnational Education. *Certification Manual.* Washington, D.C.: Global Alliance for Transnational Education, 1997.

Gubernick, L., and Ebeling, A. "I Got My Degree Through E-mail." *Forbes,* June 16, 1997, pp. 84–92.

Halal, W. E. "Creating an Entrepreneurial University: Toward a Democratic Marketplace of Ideas." *On the Horizon,* 1997, *5* (2), 1–6.

Leavitt, M. O. "Virtual U." *Multiversity,* Winter 1996, pp. 1–3.

Lundquist, J. "A Complete Transformation." *Business Officer,* 1996, *29* (12), 31–33.

MacTaggart, T. J., and Associates. *Seeking Excellence Through Independence.* San Francisco: Jossey-Bass, 1998.

Munitz, B., and Breneman, D. "Who's Who: Higher Education's Senior Leadership." *Change,* Jan./Feb. 1998, pp. 14–18.

Norris, D. M. "Fusion and the Knowledge Age." *Business Officer,* Jan. 1998, pp. 36–42.

Oblinger, D. "IBM Global Campus." *Multiversity,* Winter 1996, pp. 4–5.

O'Shea, T., Bearman, S., and Downes, A. *Quality Assurance and Assessment in Distance Learning.* Milton Keynes, U.K.: Open University Press, 1997.

Open University. *A Guide to Quality Assurance in the Open University.* Milton Keynes, U.K.: Open University Press, 1997.

Raphael, J., and Tobias, S. "Profit-Making or Profiteering?" *Change,* Nov./Dec. 1997, pp. 45–49.

Reich, R. B. "Academic Capitalism" [Review of *Academic Capitalism: Politics, Policies, and the Entrepreneurial University*]. *University Business,* Mar./Apr. 1998, pp. 65–67.

Rubin, A. M. "Webster University Strives to Become Truly International." *Chronicle of Higher Education,* July 3, 1997, pp. A43–A44.

Stapleton, L. "Twenty-Five Degrees of Separation." *TechWeek,* Feb. 1998, pp. 1–3.

Stevenson, H. H., and Gumpert, D. E. "The Heart of Entrepreneurship." *Harvard Business Review,* Mar.-Apr. 1985, pp. 85–94.

Strosnider, K. "An Aggressive, For-Profit University Challenges Traditional Colleges Nation-wide." *The Chronicle of Higher Education,* June 6, 1997, pp. A32–A33.

Strosnider, K. "For-Profit Higher Education Sees Booming Enrollments and Revenues." *The Chronicle of Higher Education,* Jan. 23, 1998, pp. A36–A38.

Traub, J. "Drive-Thru U." *The New Yorker,* Oct. 20, 1997, pp. 114–123.

Tucker, R. W. "The Rhetoric of Quality." *Adult Assessment Forum,* Summer 1997, pp. 3–7, 17.

JOHN E. NEAL is vice president for adult and professional studies at Ottawa University, Ottawa, Kansas. He previously served as dean of the School of Communications at Webster University, St. Louis, Missouri.

Recent experience indicates that the most successful quality assurance programs are initiated, maintained, and enhanced through the professional commitment of the faculty, not through quality assurance systems, administrative controls, or legislation.

The Future Dynamics of Quality Assurance: Promises and Pitfalls

Gerald H. Gaither

As the previous chapters and the editor's notes reveal, educational systems in a number of countries around the world are experimenting with programs that have at their center the idea of measuring and enhancing quality. Why this penchant for quality? The genesis of these programs has many roots, but at the core of most of them is the belief that these efforts will help the academy meet the strident demands of the public and various external agencies for more accountability, better performance, and greater efficiency and effectiveness. It has thus largely been a series of external interventions and policymakers' actions—pressures such as mass higher education and rapid enrollment growth, a perceived erosion of quality accompanying diminished resources, public demand for greater value for investments made, and government encouragement of universities to operate under more competitive market principles, among others—that has helped to bring this international movement to various nations and their institutions.

Consider a few statistics from the United States, where the proportion of eighteen- to twenty-four-year-olds enrolled in college has risen from 25 percent to 34 percent since 1980. Concomitant with this rapid growth in enrollment has been a significant rise in the cost per student of higher education, which has grown about 40 percent in inflation-adjusted dollars since 1976, outpacing enrollments. With average tuition charges rising by 80 percent in inflation-adjusted dollars since 1980, concerns about the affordability of higher education have escalated. A recent national study found that parents ranked paying for college as their second greatest fear in raising a child, behind only losing a child to a violent crime or kidnapping ("Legislators Seek Answers. . .", 1998, p. 43). On the positive side, such concerns mean that the public is convinced of education's benefits.

New Directions for Institutional Research, no. 99, Fall 1998 © Jossey-Bass Publishers

The upshot is that these excessive claims on family income, combined with increased enrollments and the diminished public dollars going to higher education, have created the dual dilemma of both lowering quality and putting a strain on the amount of education that is being purchased—an unacceptable option to both public and policymakers alike. The American public is pressuring its officials to revitalize its public colleges, to strengthen quality, and to continue to ensure broad access at reasonable cost.

Such signs of strain are also evident in many developed nations, where only the private institutions, as a general rule, have generated any significant internal pressures for reform to address these concerns. Governments, especially in the Western world, have responded to the public demand for better quality by introducing performance indicators, league tables (Great Britain), performance-based appropriations, and quality initiatives (see Gaither, Nedwek, and Neal, 1994). The historical intransigence of the academy, so eloquently captured by Clark Kerr (1987), has once again resulted in few preemptive strikes, but more often the result has been a reaction to pressures from the public, accrediting agencies, government bodies, and the like.

A few types of institutions, especially those that embrace the new electronic technologies—the "virtual" university, the "open" university, and the entrepreneurial university, among others—have been more responsive to the quality assurance movement than the traditional university. Such openness seems to occur when, following a period of rapid enrollment growth, institutions reach a certain stage of organizational maturity and subsequently seek more respectability and acceptance by mainstream academia (see Chapter Six in this volume by John Neal). The seeking of accreditation is a frequent reason for entrepreneurial institutions to embrace quality assurance methods publicly.

A number of countries seem to be following the same pattern, reining in their rapid enrollment growth in mass higher education and focusing more on the quality of the education offered. In Turkey, for example, in 1980 only 6.3 percent of the country's college-age population was enrolled in postsecondary education institutions, but in 1998 the figure is 24 percent, matching some western European countries. Enrollments increased from 237,000 in 1980 to 1.2 million in 1998. Twenty-five new institutions were established between 1992 and 1994 alone. The focus in Turkey is now on slowing enrollment growth, strengthening the new universities, improving academic quality, and moving toward institutional and programmatic accreditation (Bollag, 1998).

Is this international penchant for quality merely the latest tide of management reform to wash up on the shores of academia—succeeding such postwar experiments as PPBS (planning, programming, and budgeting systems), MBO (management by objectives), the search for excellence, and most recently, reengineering? Many of these prior waves of reform also began with great promise; their flames initially burned brightly but they soon faded away. Standing in the glow of this latest wave of reform and in the sparks of enthusiasm it has engendered, what is likely to be the fate of this movement a decade from now? Will it be another trend that was never fully digested by the academy?

Or will it take root and become a standard means by which many nations and their institutions will evaluate and constantly improve their offerings? With a few caveats outlined shortly, I believe that the quality management or quality assurance revolution, protean in nature, will have a lengthier shelf life than many of its predecessors have had.

The primary challenge, of course, is to find and disseminate meaningful ways to measure and demonstrate whether a college or university has high-quality offerings and can demonstrate that it is constantly improving the quality of the education that it provides. Despite the measurement challenges, quality assurance is one wave of reform that is unlikely to recede as easily as some of its predecessors have. It is already a crucial part of the international management reform movement that started in industry in Japan and subsequently swept through the government and education sectors, the health care industry, the service sector, and manufacturing in the Western world. Furthermore, it has gained entrance into accreditation efforts, funding initiatives, and legislation in a number of countries. The case studies in this volume have provided considerable detail on how this movement has gained the approval of policymakers, if not always of the faculty.

What can we learn from nations that have already embraced quality assurance methods? Space limitations prevent extensive discussion, but a few lessons can be noted.

First, as Kerr (1987) observed, faculties are simply going to resist internal change, especially when they cannot control the processes and the outcomes. Furthermore, because quality assurance efforts in a number of countries have come from externally mandated policies, faculties do not feel ownership of the process and exhibit a penchant for resistance rather than reform. Thus, who initiates—and who buys into—the process can make or break a system of quality assurance.

Faculty resistance may be more prescient than mere reluctance to accept change. A study by Jill MacBryde and Umit Bititci (1996) found that externally imposed quality assurance measures have built within them practices that encourage a "short termism" that endangers true quality. For example, the focus in the U.K. model, according to these authors, is on gathering statistics or providing numbers to feed short-term bureaucratic demands. Often these are simplistic measures that do not encourage the faculty to focus on long-term quality enhancement that complements their organization's objectives. These authors also believe—as I do—that institutions can address quality, but they must do so through a focus on customer satisfaction.

But herein lies the dilemma. If faculty are going to resist any change, and are uncomfortable being judged—as we all are—how then can quality assurance methods be implemented? First, as institutional researchers have long known, faculty ownership of the data, the process, or both stimulates greater acceptance of the results and leads to appropriate actions. Second, the system should develop quality assurance measures that are easy to assess, such as graduation rates, retention, and student satisfaction, and that are valid and reliable.

Another secret to success is to focus on the positive rather than the negative, to reward success rather than penalize failure, and to earmark certain monies for individual (as opposed to institutional) incentive bonuses for faculty who meet or exceed state, institutional, or self-defined standards and goals. As noted at the outset of this volume, academic quality is best maintained and enhanced through the professional commitment of the faculty, and should be viewed primarily as a professional issue. Quality maintenance and enhancement is not an external political or internal administrative function, although administrative leadership can be vital. Any external body that adds another layer of bureaucratic accountability to faculty who already view themselves as overworked, underappreciated, and underpaid is not likely to receive a warm welcome—even if the administration is concerned about explaining and defending the institution to a variety of external constituencies.

Timing and patience are also key elements. Elected officials often want immediate implementation and results and resort to what Peter Ewell has labeled "legislation by fax," incorporating rapid innovation but neglecting to adapt prescribed systems to local circumstances (see Gaither, Nedwek, and Neal, 1994). Colleges and universities need time to adopt measures and adapt them to their particular environments and missions, and they need adequate time to digest the process. It is not unheard of for politicians to adopt a system one year and want results by the next. Such processes create cynicism in the affected parties, and resistance rather than reform is the result. As MacBryde and Bititci (1996) found, the collection of statistics takes priority over improving quality, and the goals become distorted by the detail. Burton Clark (1994) has concluded from an international study that a "central bureaucracy cannot effectively coordinate higher education" (p. 14). Strong counter forces must be brought into play to shift responsibility from a central authority to the university. As noted earlier, changing the reward system to enhance results through professional commitment is one productive way that policymakers can positively add to both the debate about quality and efforts to enhance it.

The quality movement is best understood as evolving from the cumulative effects of past indiscretions and lapses in assuming the public mantle of accountability. These same conditions will continue to shape higher education's future, whatever the nation. I believe that the ambience of reform reflected in this comparative volume provides lessons for helping to avoid some of the more unwanted and unanticipated consequences of the quality assurance movement and to gain from its best efforts.

As a concluding observation, these pages suggest that although cultures and values may differ across nations and although institutions are at different stages of development in their quality assurance programs, their problems, processes, and indeed even political responses are more similar than dissimilar. As a result, this comparative, international perspective has allowed the five nations discussed to contribute richly to a network of quality assurance methods that offers valuable lessons for all higher education systems, whatever the nation.

References

Bollag, B. "Turkey Focuses on Improving the Quality of Public Universities." *Chronicle of Higher Education,* 1998, *44* (34), A57.

Clark, B. R. "The Insulated Americans: Lessons from Abroad." In P. Altbach, R. Berdahl, and P. Gumport (eds.), *Higher Education in American Society.* (3rd ed.). Amherst, N.Y.: Prometheus Books, 1994.

Gaither, G., Nedwek, B. and Neal, J. *Measuring Up: The Promises and Pitfalls of Performance Indications in Higher Education.* ASHE-ERIC Higher Education Report Five. Washington, D.C.: George Washington University, Graduate School of Education and Human Development, 1994.

Kerr, C. "A Critical Age in the University World: Accumulated Heritage Versus Modern Imperatives." *European Journal of Education,* 1987, *22* (2), 183–193.

"Legislators Seek Answers to Rising Price of College." *Houston Chronicle,* May 3, 1998, p. 43.

MacBryde, J. C., and Bititci, U. S. "Quality Management in Higher Education: A Double-Edged Sword." Paper presented at the European Foundation for Quality Management Seventh Conference: Learning Edge, Paris, Apr. 24–26, 1996. [http://www.strath.ac.uk/Departments/DMEM/CSM/ paperl.htm]. Accessed Apr. 27, 1998.

GERALD H. GAITHER *is director of institutional effectiveness, research, and analysis at the Prairie View A&M University campus of the Texas A&M University System.*

The materials cited in this chapter are based on recent scholarship and materials available through the new electronic technologies. They provide an international collection of practical sources for dealing with quality assurance issues.

Quality Assurance in Higher Education: A Selective Resource Guide

Anthony J. Adam, Malcolm Morrison

The literature on the quality assurance (QA) and total quality management (TQM) movements in higher education has exploded in the 1990s, and the following resource list makes no attempt even to be remotely comprehensive. Our list includes both books and Web sites. The sources cited can lead to more comprehensive bibliographies, including articles, pamphlets, and conference proceedings. For updates on literature in the field, we recommend the ERIC database (search on "quality assurance" and "higher education"), The Center for Quality Assurance in International Education (http://www.edugate.org), and the journal *Quality Assurance in Education* (see later). In addition, the chapters in this volume have cited other valuable references.

Bogue, E. G., and Saunders, R. L. *The Evidence for Quality: Strengthening the Tests of Academic and Administrative Effectiveness.* San Francisco: Jossey-Bass, 1992.

Quality in higher education can be defined, measured, and used to inform academic decision making in a variety of ways. The authors of this book propose a definition of quality and proceed to examine, with case study examples, current approaches to QA in the United States, including accreditation, student feedback studies, professional licensure, academic program review, and outcomes assessment. The emerging role of state agencies in QA and enhancement is discussed, and the authors conclude by offering an integrated QA model that addresses accountability and improvement for student services, programs, and assessment.

Bowden, J. A., and Sachs, J. (eds.). "Managing the Quality of University Learning and Teaching: The Eltham Symposium," June 1997. [http://www.deetya.gov.au/divisions/hed/operations/Bowden/front.html]. Accessed Nov. 21, 1997.

This report, produced under the auspices of the Commonwealth of Australia's Department of Employment, Education, Training, and Youth Affairs (DEETYA) Higher Education office, includes international reports on such diverse topics as contextualizing quality in Australian universities in the 1990s, implementation of QA policies and procedures in the United States, continual quality improvement in learning and teaching, and developing a QA system. Very good on-line resource for all researchers.

Brennan, J., de Vries, P., and Williams, R. (eds.). *Standards and Quality in Higher Education*. London: Jessica Kingsley, 1997.

This book contains perspectives on academic standards and QA in higher education from nine countries and three contrasting vantage points: national and state agencies (including those in France, New Zealand, the United Kingdom, and the United States), higher education institutions (in Australia, Denmark, and Sweden) and international organizations (such as the OECD-funded Institutional Management in Higher Education, or IMHE, project investigating quality management, quality assessment, and the decision-making process in higher education). The articles address current issues, including the State Postsecondary Review Entity (SPRE) legislation and institutional accreditation in the United States, the U.K. debate on academic standards, and the impact in Australia of national quality audit exercises conducted by the Committee for Quality Assurance in Higher Education. In his introduction, Brennan identifies controversies about the language of quality, power, and ownership of the quality process, and the use of quality judgments to promote and respond to accelerating change in higher education. The book does not seek to advocate any one approach to quality but usefully clarifies in a wider context the difficult issues and choices faced by QA policymakers and practitioners.

Commission of the European Communities. *Quality Management and Quality Assurance in European Higher Education* (Education Training Youth Studies No. 1). Luxembourg: Office for Official Publications of the European Communities, 1993.

This is an excellent introduction to QA as practiced by European Union member nations, with special focus on the differences between traditions in the United Kingdom and on the European continent, on quality assessment and audits in practice in select nations, and on the use of performance indicators. National progress reports on QA are also included.

Commonwealth of Australia, Department of Employment, Education, Training and Youth Affairs Higher Education Division Quality Assurance, July 16, 1997 [http://www.deetya.gov.au/divisions/hed/highered/quality.htm]. Accessed Nov. 21, 1997.

DEETYA's QA Web site is a central unit for locating all related higher education reports in the Commonwealth of Australia since 1994. Some of the entries have clickable links to complete documents, although the majority are only brief citations. There is much potential here, as more universities load their reports and offer links.

Ellis, R. (ed.). *Quality Assurance for University Teaching*. Buckingham, U.K.: Society for Research into Higher Education and Open University Press, 1993.
    This book presents QA from a U.K. perspective, based on three themes: assuring, identifying, and developing quality. There is a strong emphasis on actual practice, including the application of a British standard of measurement and evaluation to an institution's quest for TQM, and the embedding of course validation and review, student evaluations, and institutional research in an institution's QA policies and procedures. Characteristics of quality teaching and learning are highlighted in chapters on professional models for quality, teaching styles of award-winning professors, and staff development issues. Ellis's introductory chapter on issues and approaches is an excellent starting point for defining QA in relation to quality control, quality audit, and quality assessment.

Folger, J. K., and Harris, J. W. *Assessment in Accreditation*. Report sponsored by a grant from the Fund for the Improvement of Postsecondary Education. Decatur, Ga.: Southern Association of Colleges and Schools, 1989.
    Written primarily for institutions in the Southern Association of Colleges and Schools, a U.S. accrediting body, this study outlines the background of assessment and quality improvement at universities, discusses the self-study process as it relates to changing accreditation requirements, and finally presents three case studies of the development of the assessment process at universities. Very useful for both the campus administrator and accreditation team member.

Freed, J. E. *A Culture for Academic Excellence: Implementing the Quality Principles in Higher Education*. ASHE-ERIC Higher Education Report, Vol. 25, No. 1. Washington, D.C.: Graduate School of Education and Human Development, George Washington University, 1997. (ED 406 963)
    This work presents a good overview of how quality principles can work within a holistic system to improve the higher education process. Not much is new in this lengthy report to practitioners, but Freed's viewpoint is that of a business professor and therefore offers an outsider's view of how quality should be approached. The report contains an extensive bibliography.

Green, D. (ed.). *What Is Quality in Higher Education?* Buckingham, U.K.: Society for Research into Higher Education and Open University Press, 1994.
    This book is a collection of articles written from a U.K. perspective before the quality assessment requirements of the 1992 Further and Higher Education Act were implemented. Topics include defining and measuring the quality of teaching and learning, the direct observation of quality in the classroom by an external agency, quality audit (the external examination of

an institution's QA procedures and practices), quality models from other public sector and commercial organizations, and an international perspective on QA embracing ten countries, including the United States, Hong Kong, the Netherlands, and Australia.

Grotelueschen, A. D. *Quality Assurance in Continuing Professional Education.* Athens, Ga.: Adult Education Department, College of Education, University of Georgia, 1986.

This book discusses methods of evaluating services and teaching methods for QA in continuing professional education programs. The author presents a Likertype seven-point scale for rating instructional method, course content, participant benefits, setting, and other facets of the programs. A useful if brief practical methodology focusing more on quality assessment than on assurance.

Higher Education Funding Council for England [http://www.hefce.ac.uk]. Accessed June 2, 1998.

The Higher Education Funding Council distributes funds provided by the secretary of state for education and employment to 136 universities and higher education colleges in England, and under the 1992 Further and Higher Education Act has a statutory obligation to assess the quality of education in those institutions, an activity commonly known as *teaching quality assessment.* Detailed reports on the quality of education on a subject basis at each institution are available at the Web site following the phased assessment of all sixty-one subjects from 1993–2001 (more than a thousand such reports on forty-two subjects are currently published). The site also includes outcome of the 1992 and 1996 Research Assessment Exercises for English institutions, and circulars, briefings, and other papers published since 1994. The site provides links to related organizations, including the Quality Assurance Agency, established in 1997 as the successor organization to the Higher Education Quality Council.

Higher Education Funding Council for Wales [http://www.niss.ac.uk/education/hefcw/]. Accessed June 2, 1998.

The Higher Education Funding Council for Wales distributes funds provided by the secretary of state for Wales to thirteen higher education institutions in Wales. It has the same statutory obligation to assess the quality of education as its sister agencies in England (the Higher Education Funding Council for England, or HEFCE) and Scotland (the Scottish Higher Education Funding Council) and has completed a program of subject-based assessment at each institution from 1993–1998. A summary of the outcome of the assessment program, both by institution and by subject, is given at the Web site. Detailed reports, however, are not available (unlike at the HEFCE's site). Other documents include circulars and publications available since 1995 that are similar to those available at the sister sites for England and Scotland.

Higher Education Quality Council [http://www.niss.ac.uk/education/heqc/]. Accessed June 2, 1998.

The Higher Education Quality Council (HEQC) was established in 1992 as a wholly independent, limited company funded by subscription by U.K. higher education institutions. Its mission is to provide public assurance and accountability for the maintenance and enhancement of academic quality and standards. From 1992 to 1997, HEQC conducted a program of quality audit visits to every higher education institution in the United Kingdom, publishing a public report on each visit. Although texts of these reports are not available at the Web site, price and ordering information is provided both for the reports and for an extensive range of QA guidelines and codes of practice published by the HEQC. In July 1997, the responsibilities of the HEQC were transferred to the new Quality Assurance Agency for Higher Education (QAA). At the time of this writing, the HEQC Web site can still be accessed, but in the long term the texts are likely to be relocated on the QAA site.

Illinois State Board of Higher Education. *Illinois Public Universities Priorities, Quality, and Productivity Executive Summaries.* Springfield: Illinois State Board of Higher Education, 1996. (ED 400 770)

This publication is one in a series of documents focusing on one state's effort to coordinate quality and productivity at systemwide and statewide levels. The IBHE initiative Priorities, Quality, and Productivity was expanded after initial discussions in the early 1990s to include examinations of faculty roles and responsibilities, resource allocation management, and budgetary and reinvestment opportunities for public and private colleges and universities. Interesting related documents are available from ERIC on collecting faculty data statewide (ED 400 767) and on proprietary institutions (ED 400 769).

Institutional Quality Assurance Program, U.S. Dept. of Education [http:// sfa.ed. gov]. Accessed Nov. 26, 1997.

The Quality Assurance Program provides postsecondary institutions in the United States with a framework for conducting a continuous process of quality improvements in the delivery of Title IV programs. Eighty-seven institutions participated in the program in the 1994–95 program year, monitoring the distribution of student financial aid packages and avoiding approximately $89 million in overpayments. Very little documentation is provided at this or related institutional sites.

Kogan, M. (ed.). *Evaluating Higher Education.* London: Jessica Kingsley Publishers, 1989.

This book is a collection of papers from the *International Journal of Institutional Management in Higher Education.* It presents a EuroAmerican perspective on quality assessment, assurance, and accountability. It includes articles on allocation of public funds based on instructional performance and quality indicators, on evaluating institutions in the United States and France, on the basics of faculty evaluation and peer review, and on the place of university research in the evaluation process.

Marcus, L. R. *The Path to Excellence: Quality Assurance in Higher Education.* ASHE-ERIC Higher Education Research Report No. 1. Washington, D.C.: Association for the Study of Higher Education, ERIC Clearinghouse on Higher Education, 1983. (ED 227 800)

Marcus posits that for institutions of higher education to practice QA, both process and outcome orientations are required to be part of the program assessment. Readers should pay closest attention to the final section, "Ensuring Academic Quality through Self-Regulation," which outlines quantitative and qualitative factors that affect academic evaluation. An excellent and extensive bibliography is appended.

Master of Science Degree in Quality Assurance [http://www.msqa.edu/]. Accessed Nov. 19, 1997.

In an exemplary conjunction of all elements on this topic, Southern Polytechnic State University (a nationally accredited university in the University System of Georgia) now offers its QA master's degree over the Internet. Students can register, take classes and seminars, access the Web (unfortunately labeled "Library Access"), and link to related sites, including the American Society for Quality's Web site. The degree itself is designed for engineering technology majors, but the Web adaptation should be of interest to any administrator or faculty member seeking innovative teaching methods.

Monash University Quality Portfolio, Oct. 30, 1995 [http://www.monash.edu.au/resgrant/quality/]. Accessed Dec. 2, 1997.

This review document covers evaluations from a quality perspective on research and research training, with breakdowns on management, income, and outcomes. Most interesting from a practical perspective are the summaries of faculty research management plans, arranged by department.

Piper, D. W. *Quality Management in Universities.* Canberra: Australian Government Publishing Service, 1993.

This highly practical guidebook for outlining QA procedures is based on practices at Australian universities. The author's no-nonsense approach covers principals of quality management, criteria for judging the merit of systems overall, and the relationship of quality audits to government funding. The procedural frameworks presented are invaluable to university administrators.

Quality Advancement at the University of Otago Web page, Sept. 25, 1997 [http://www.otago.ac.nz/Web_menus/Dept_Homepages/Quality/home.html]. Accessed Dec. 3, 1997.

This Web site includes sections on quality principles, strategies for managing change, departmental and program reviews, academic audits, and a bibliography of high-quality reference material on the topic. Information is in outline form in some of the sections, but still useful overall.

Quality Assurance Agency for Higher Education [http://www.niss.ac.uk/education/qaa/]. Accessed June 2, 1998.

The Quality Assurance Agency was established in 1997 to develop a single QA framework for U.K. higher education, taking over the teaching quality assessment responsibilities of the U.K. funding councils and all the functions of the former Higher Education Quality Council (HEQC). Its major task is to develop and implement new QA arrangements during 1998–2001 in response to the 1997 Dearing Report. Its Web site is at an early stage of preparation and currently contains a key consultation document on the agency's proposals to provide public assurance of the quality and standards of U.K. higher education. It also provides a link to the former HEQC. The site will become the main reference point for QA policy developments in U.K. higher education.

Quality Assurance at the University of Tampere [http://www.uta.fi/opiskelu/opla/]. Accessed Nov. 4, 1997.

Based primarily on work instituted in 1994 and 1995 at the Finnish University of Tampere, this site includes basic information on the quality assurance unit (QAU) established in 1996, its relationship with the Finnish Higher Education Evaluation Council, and current activities of the QAU. This is a good example of Scandinavian QA efforts.

Quality Assurance in Education [http://www.mcb.co.uk/cgibin/journal1/qae]. Accessed Nov. 20, 1997.

This rather expensive scholarly journal (U.S. $950+), published since 1993 by MCB University Press, aims to examine critically quality and related issues in education, to bridge the gap between theory and practice in all aspects of QA, and to provide practical assistance to administrators and researchers. Articles address a wide audience and include attention to implementing procedures and setting up an evaluative framework. At the Web site, users can browse the contents of individual issues, but abstracts and other access are available only to subscribers.

Quality Plaza, Aug. 31, 1997 [http://www.hk.super.net/~williamw/quality.html]. Accessed Nov. 6, 1997.

One of the largest of all TQM and QA Web sites, this Hong Kong–based collection offers the researcher texts in all aspects of the field, including TQM, ISO 9000 and 14000, zero quality control, costs, best practices, and continuous improvement. It provides a nearly comprehensive list of links to worldwide QA organizations, resource guides, magazines, and so on, and is an excellent starting point for novices and advanced searchers alike.

Romer, R. *Making Quality Count in Undergraduate Education: A Report for the ECS Chairman's "Quality Counts" Agenda in Higher Education.* Denver, Colo.: Education Commission of the States, 1995. (ED 388 208)

Former Colorado Governor Roy Romer served as chairman of the Education Commission of the States (ECS) in 1994–95 and chose "quality counts" as his theme. He notes that for QA to work, system heads and state officials must work closely together to achieve common but achievable goals, particularly in regard to state priorities. Officials must also link quality and accountability at all levels. Quality may be measured in terms of quantitative state-level student consumer-information indicators, although some variables are unmeasurable.

Rutgers University Program for Organizational Quality and Communication Improvement, Oct. 1, 1997 [http://www.scils.rutgers.edu/qci/ci.html]. Accessed Nov. 6, 1997.

Established in 1993 to provide leadership in organizational effectiveness, the Program for Organizational Quality and Communication Improvement offers general information on QA in a university setting, with special programs in a variety of areas (such as workplace climate and service excellence). Primarily in outline form, this site is useful predominantly for covering basic issues as they relate to higher education.

Scottish Higher Education Funding Council [http://www.shefc.ac.uk/shefc/welcome.html]. Accessed June 2, 1998.

The Scottish Higher Education Funding Council distributes funds provided by the secretary of state for Scotland to twenty-one higher education institutions in Scotland. It has the same statutory obligation to assess the quality of education as its sister agencies in England (the Higher Education Funding Council for England) and Wales (the Higher Education Funding Council for Wales) and, as has the Wales agency, it has completed a program of subject-based assessment at each institution during 1992–1998. Detailed reports and a summary of the outcomes of this assessment program are available at the Web site. Other documents available include the outcome of the 1992 and 1996 research assessment exercises for Scottish institutions, the 1997 Dearing/Garrick Report ("Higher Education in the Learning Society"), and other circulars and publications similar to those available at the sister sites for England and Wales.

Suarez, J. G. *Three Experts on Quality Management: Philip B. Crosby, W. Edwards Deming, Joseph M. Juran.* Total Quality Leadership Office Publication no. 9202, July 1992 [http://deming.eng.clemson.edu/pub/psci/files/3expert.txt]. Accessed Nov. 4, 1997.

Published for the U.S. Department of the Navy's Total Quality Leadership Office, this report concisely compares and contrasts the TQM theories of TQM's three leading proponents. An excellent starting point for any administrator seeking basic points from the experts.

University of Dundee Quality Advisory Unit [http://www.dundee.ac.uk/Quality/]. Accessed Nov. 26, 1997.

This site provides a gateway to Scottish Higher Education Funding Council reports by subject field. Possibly of more interest is the students' guide to QA procedures for teaching and learning, which consists of brochures on program review, academic standards, new course approval, student participation in audits, and other areas of student interest. It is an excellent example of how one institution keeps students informed on QA issues.

University of East London Quality Assurance Department home page [http://www.uel.ac.uk/non-academic/qa/info.html]. Accessed Dec. 2, 1997.
    This detailed Web site includes the department's own service standards, appeals and complaints procedures, QA principles and system overview, monitoring and evaluation, and the student feedback process. Much good material is provided for institutions interested in organizing similar units.

University of Glasgow Quality Assurance Office, Nov. 6, 1997 [http://www.gla.ac.uk/Otherdepts/Quality/]. Accessed Dec. 2, 1997.
    Most useful at this Web site is the *Quality Assurance of Teaching Guide to Good Practice* (currently under review), which provides detailed information on course information documentation, student feedback, external examiners, course review, and student support mechanisms.

University of Liverpool Quality Assurance Unit, Dec. 1, 1997 [http://www.liv.ac.uk/qau/qau.html]. Accessed Dec. 2, 1997.
    This is an excellent site in terms of both type of information presented and its organization, with reports on standards of service for the QA unit, internal QA policies and procedures, external QA controls, annual course monitoring procedures, and links to external organizations and sites (such as the Higher Education Funding Council for England). Also provides material published by the Office for Standards in Education.

The University of Texas Quality Center, Aug. 29, 1997 [http://www.utexas.edu/admin/utqc/]. Accessed Nov. 5, 1997.
    This organization provides TQM training for businesses, nonprofits, and educational institutions in the state of Texas, with courses on team building, tools and techniques, and so on. Its Web site is most useful for links to QA sites, including the Quality Management Consortia, Hong Kong's Quality Plaza, and the Higher Education Processes Network.

The University of Western Australia 1995 Quality Assurance Portfolio, Sept. 22, 1995 [http://www.acs.uwa.edu.au/www_serv/research/policy/qr/main.html]. Accessed Nov. 21, 1997.
    This complete source document for the 1995 study (the latest available on the Web) includes sections on the university budget, research policy and management, and community services, with extensive statistical appendices. It is an excellent model for campus QA planning bodies.

Victoria University of Wellington (VUW), Academic Audit Unit Papers and Quality Assuranc/e Provisions, Aug. 29, 1997 [http://www.vuw.ac.nz/administrative/]. Accessed Nov. 4, 1997.

This site includes academic audit unit papers from the New Zealand Universities Academic Audit Unit; Quality Assurance Provisions, 1996; the general report of VUW's academic audit unit (July 1996); and peripheral reports on restructuring and governance of VUW. The site provides excellent practical guidelines for establishing a QA unit on university campuses.

ANTHONY J. ADAM is a reference librarian in the J. B. Coleman Library at Prairie View A&M University, Prairie View, Texas.

MALCOLM MORRISON is the academic registrar at the Cranfield University, Bedfordshire, England.

INDEX

Back Issue/Subscription Order Form

Copy or detach and send to:
Jossey-Bass Inc., Publishers, 350 Sansome Street, San Francisco CA 94104-1342
Call or fax toll free!
Phone 888-378-2537 6AM-5PM PST; Fax 800-605-2665

Back issues   Please send me the following issues at $23 each:
                                (Important: please include series initials and issue number, such as IR90)

1. IR _____

_____

_____

$ _____ Total for single issues

$ _____ Shipping charges (for single issues ***only;*** subscriptions are exempt
from shipping charges): Up to $30, add $5^{50} • $30^{01}–$50, add $6^{50}
$50^{01}–$75, add $7^{50} • $75^{01}–$100, add $9 • $100^{01}–$150, add $10
Over $150, call for shipping charge

Subscriptions   Please ❑ start   ❑ renew my subscription to *New Directions
for Institutional Reseach* for the year 19___ at the following rate:

❑ Individual $56   ❑ Institutional $95
NOTE: Subscriptions are quarterly, and are for the calendar year only.
Subscriptions begin with the spring issue of the year indicated above.
For shipping outside the U.S., please add $25.

$ _____ Total single issues and subscriptions (CA, IN, NJ, NY and DC
residents, add sales tax for single issues. NY and DC residents must
include shipping charges when calculating sales tax. NY and Canadian
residents only, add sales tax for subscriptions.)

❑ Payment enclosed (U.S. check or money order only)

❑ VISA, MC, AmEx, Discover Card #_____ Exp. date_____

Signature _____ Day phone _____

❑ Bill me (U.S. institutional orders only. Purchase order required.)

Purchase order #_____

Name _____

Address _____

_____

Phone_____ E-mail _____

For more information about Jossey-Bass Publishers, visit our Web site at:
www.josseybass.com   **PRIORITY CODE = ND1**